FLOYD CLYMER'S MOTORCYCLIST'S LIBRARY

The Second Book of the
ROYAL ENFIELD

COMPREHENSIVE RIDING AND MAINTENANCE INSTRUCTIONS FOR OWNERS OF 1958–66 250 C.C., 1963–65 350 C.C. "CRUSADER" TYPE SINGLES HAVING UNIT CONSTRUCTION OF ENGINE AND GEARBOX

BY

W. C. HAYCRAFT

F.R.S.A.

ANNOUNCEMENT

By special arrangement with the original publishers of this book, Sir Isaac Pitman & Son, Ltd., of London, England, we have secured the exclusive publishing rights for this book, as well as all others in THE MOTORCYCLIST'S LIBRARY.

Included in THE MOTORCYCLIST'S LIBRARY are complete instruction manuals covering the care and operation of respective motorcycles and engines; valuable data on speed tuning, and thrilling accounts of motorcycle race events. See listing of available titles elsewhere in this edition.

We consider it a privilege to be able to offer so many fine titles to our customers.

FLOYD CLYMER
Publisher of Books Pertaining to Automobiles and Motorcycles

2125 W. PICO ST.   LOS ANGELES 6, CALIF.

E.S. MOTORS
LIMITED
The Specialists for

YOUR NEW
Royal Enfield
GO ON A   GT
CONTINENTAL   SUPER
250 c.c.

TOP EXCHANGE ALLOWANCE
EASY CONFIDENTIAL H.P. TERMS

ALWAYS A GRAND SELECTION OF
GUARANTEED USED MODELS
UNRIVALLED PER RETURN
C.O.D. SERVICE for
SPARES and ACCESSORIES
319-325 High Road, Chiswick, London, W.4
Telephone: CHIswick 6368-Sales, 2246-Spares

INTRODUCTION

Welcome to the world of digital publishing ~ the book you now hold in your hand, while unchanged from the original edition, was printed using the latest state of the art digital technology. The advent of print-on-demand has forever changed the publishing process, never has information been so accessible and it is our hope that this book serves your informational needs for years to come. If this is your first exposure to digital publishing, we hope that you are pleased with the results. Many more titles of interest to the classic automobile and motorcycle enthusiast, collector and restorer are available via our website at www.VelocePress.com. We hope that you find this title as interesting as we do.

NOTE FROM THE PUBLISHER

The information presented is true and complete to the best of our knowledge. All recommendations are made without any guarantees on the part of the author or the publisher, who also disclaim all liability incurred with the use of this information.

TRADEMARKS

We recognize that some words, model names and designations, for example, mentioned herein are the property of the trademark holder. We use them for identification purposes only. This is not an official publication.

INFORMATION ON THE USE OF THIS PUBLICATION

This manual is an invaluable resource for the classic motorcycle enthusiast and a "must have" for owners interested in performing their own maintenance. However, in today's information age we are constantly subject to changes in common practice, new technology, availability of improved materials and increased awareness of chemical toxicity. As such, it is advised that the user consult with an experienced professional prior to undertaking any procedure described herein. While every care has been taken to ensure correctness of information, it is obviously not possible to guarantee complete freedom from errors or omissions or to accept liability arising from such errors or omissions. Therefore, any individual that uses the information contained within, or elects to perform or participate in do-it-yourself repairs or modifications acknowledges that there is a risk factor involved and that the publisher or its associates cannot be held responsible for personal injury or property damage resulting from the use of the information or the outcome of such procedures.

WARNING!

One final word of advice, this publication is intended to be used as a reference guide, and when in doubt the reader should consult with a qualified technician.

PREFACE

The 1958–66 250 c.c. and 1963–5 350 c.c. single-cylinder O.H.V. four-stroke Royal Enfields dealt with in this handbook are all basically of the same "Crusader" design employing unit construction of the engine and gearbox and with the oil tank integral with the crankcase. Their design differs greatly from that of the earlier 1946–62 models having the engine separate from the gearbox. Their maintenance is covered in another handbook in this series.

The 250 c.c. "Crusader Sports" is a typical example of the most attractive-looking 1958–66 range. It combines proved reliability and a small thirst for petrol (about 95 m.p.g.) with exhilarating acceleration, precise steering, and a full-throttle top speed of no less than 75–80 m.p.h.

A 250 c.c. Royal Enfield which deserves special praise is the 1965–6 "Continental G.T." model which besides having a superb performance and low fuel consumption, has a most alluring sporty look (*see* page 2). It has proved so exciting to young enthusiasts that its rate of production has outstripped that of all other 250 c.c. machines now manufactured at Redditch.

Reliability, economical running, high performance are pleasing characteristics of 1958–66 machines. To preserve these characteristics they all deserve careful maintenance.

The primary purpose of this handbook is to provide in a clear and non-technical manner *all essential maintenance instructions* necessary to keep your mount in first-class running condition, to reduce its annual depreciation to the minimum, and to enable you for years to obtain the maximum pleasure, mileage, m.p.g., m.p.h. and m.p.£ from it. Chapter I is intended for newcomers to motor-cycling and those who have never previously ridden a "Crusader" type Royal Enfield. The advice about running-in and safe riding should be particularly noted and put into practice. The remaining chapters deal very thoroughly with the proper maintenance of the power unit and motor-cycle, but not with major overhaul which for several reasons (*see* page 89) is beyond the average motor-cyclist.

Note that *all instructions, except where otherwise stated, apply to all* 250, 350 *c.c. models dealt with in this handbook.* These models are—

1. The 1958–62 "Crusader 250."
2. The 1959–66 250 c.c. "Crusader Sports."
3. The 1962–3 250 c.c. "Crusader Super 5."
4. The 1958–65 "250 Clipper."

PREFACE

5. The 1963-5 "350 Bullet."
6. The 1963-5 250 c.c. "Continental."
7. The 1965 250 c.c. "Olympic."
8. The 1955-6 250 c.c. "Continental G.T."

In conclusion the author sincerely thanks The Enfield Cycle Company Ltd. of Redditch for kindly supplying useful technical data and for according him permission to reproduce various copyright drawings. Their Service Manager has kindly checked over the proofs of this book for technical accuracy. Some sketches have been carefully annotated by the author to increase their practical value. Thanks are also given to E. S. Motors Ltd. of Chiswick, London, W.4, and to Amal Ltd. and Joseph Lucas Ltd. of Birmingham for their assistance.

BEDFORD ROW, W. C. HAYCRAFT
   WORTHING,
     SUSSEX

CONTENTS

CHAP.   PAGE

I. HANDLING YOUR MOUNT   1
Preliminaries—Layout and use of controls—Gear changing—Running-in—Advice on safety

II. THE AMAL CARBURETTOR 15
"Monobloc" carburettor details—Adjustment and faults—Carburettor maintenance—The air filter

III. CORRECT LUBRICATION 26
Engine lubrication—The motor-cycle parts

IV. LUCAS A.C. LIGHTING-IGNITION 38
The system explained—The alternator and rectifier—Battery maintenance—The lamps—The Lucas electric horn—The ignition system—Maintenance of ignition system—Ignition timing (all models)

V. GENERAL MAINTENANCE 59
Spares and repairs—Cleaning engine and machine—Miscellaneous—Valve clearances—The timing and primary chains—The dry-sump system—Decarbonizing and valve grinding—Ignition and valve timing—Dismantling, replacing the cam gear—Major engine overhaul—The gearbox—The clutch—Transmission chains—The cush-drive—Care of tyres—Brake maintenance—Front and rear wheels—Steering-head adjustment—Front and rear suspension

Index 119

CHAPTER I

HANDLING YOUR MOUNT

This chapter is intended mainly for the benefit of novices and deals with the actual handling of your mount rather than the technique of riding and the cultivation of road sense. It is assumed that you are the owner of a brand new four-stroke single-cylinder O.H.V. model or have just bought a good second-hand machine and are anxious to get on the road. The first step is to buy some good protective clothing, leather gauntlets, and a crash helmet. It is not compulsory to wear a crash helmet but the author advises you to wear one *always* while riding. With modern traffic conditions even the most experienced and careful rider can meet with an accident through no fault of his own. Accidents to motor-cyclists often involve head contact with the road or with the other vehicle concerned and if a crash helmet is not worn the most disastrous consequences may follow. Obtain a copy of *The Highway Code* and read and digest its contents most thoroughly. It contains very sound advice.

Essential Legal Preliminaries. If you are under 16 you are *not* permitted to ride *any* type of motor-cycle. Before you can legally get on the road astride a brand new or second-hand Royal Enfield you must comply with certain legal preliminaries. Various forms can be obtained from a money-order Post Office and must be carefully and truthfully filled in. Note and comply with the following—
 1. If you own a second-hand machine make sure that it is in a thoroughly roadworthy condition. Pay special attention to the tyres, brakes, steering, lights, horn, speedometer, etc. It is now an offence to ride a machine on the public highway which is not in a roadworthy condition.
 2. Take out an insurance policy to cover all *third-party* risks, and see that you obtain the all-important "Certificate of Insurance." Where a new machine is concerned you cannot obtain the certificate until the machine has been registered and a registration number allocated to it. An insurance "cover note" can be obtained prior to the issue of the certificate. If you buy a Royal Enfield on hire-purchase terms, you will almost certainly be required to take out a full comprehensive insurance policy. Where a valuable machine is concerned, it is always best to take out such a policy.
 3. Obtain a registration book and registration licence. If your machine is new or has changed hands, fill up Form R.F. 1/2. If you wish to *renew* your registration licence, fill up Form R.F. 1/A. The registration fee (£8 and £4 per annum for 350 c.c. and 250 c.c. solo models respectively)

must always be accompanied by a "Certificate of Insurance" or a "cover note" and the engine and frame numbers must be stated on Form R.F. 1/2. The engine number will be found stamped on the driving side of the

FIG. 1. A RELIABLE AND TOUGH 248 C.C. SPORTS MOUNT WITH A CAPACITY FOR HARD WORK AND HIGH SPEED AT LOW M.P.G.—THE 1965–6 "CONTINENTAL G.T." ROYAL ENFIELD

Its specification includes: a "Crusader" type engine with coil ignition to ensure easy starting; an Amal "monobloc" carburettor; a sports-type exhaust pipe; a race-proved fibre-glass petrol tank; a five-speed gearbox; a race-styled dualseat; large polished front-hub flanges; polished aluminium mudguards, chromed rear suspension springs; and a sports windscreen. This very sporty-looking model will attain 80–85 m.p.h., run normally at about 90 m.p.g., and weighs only 300 lb. The remaining 1966 "Crusader"-type single is the 248 c.c. "Crusader Sports" (see Preface and Fig. 56) introduced in 1959. The somewhat less sporty "250 Clipper" introduced in 1958 was discontinued after 1965

(*The Enfield Cycle Co. Ltd.*)

crankcase below the cylinder barrel. The frame number is located at the top of the front down-tube or head lug.

4. Keep the registration book in a safe place and return it to the registration authorities for amendment if you change your address or sell the machine. Insert the registration licence disc in a waterproof holder (facing the near side) attached to the handlebars, the front down-tube, or the telescopic front forks.

5. If you are a "learner" take out a "provisional" driving licence which is valid for six months and costs 10s. It can be renewed as required and the application form for each licence is Form D.L.1. Sign the driving licence. Attach "L" plates to the front and rear of the machine if you

Fig. 2. The Smart Royal Enfield "Sportsflow" Fairing—An Ideal Extra for All-weather Riders

This fairing gives superb weather protection and is aerodynamically designed to increase road performance and slightly reduce petrol consumption. It can be quickly fitted to any 250 c.c. "Crusader"-type model except the 1965–6 "Continental G.T." model and is available in different colours for matching purposes. For owners of 350 c.c. machines an "Airflow" fairing is available. This can also be specified as original equipment on all current models except the 1965–6 "Continental G.T." model

(*The Enfield Cycle Co. Ltd.*)

are a "learner." The "L" plates must not obscure the index letters or registration numbers. "Provisional" licence holders must not ride machines over 250 c.c.

6. If you are a "learner" and feel qualified to take a driving test, make application on Form D.L.26. A driving test costs £1.

7. While you are a "learner" you must not carry a pillion passenger unless he or she has a "full" three-year current driving licence.

8. If you are qualified to ride without "L" plates and have passed a

driving test, apply on Form D.L.1. for a "full" three-year driving licence. It costs 15s. Sign the driving licence as soon as you get it.

9. Always see that your speedometer and horn are in proper working order. Also be sure that your speedometer and rear number plate are easily read by night as well as by day. The speedometer, by the way, must show within ±10 per cent accuracy when 30 m.p.h. is being exceeded.

LAYOUT AND USE OF CONTROLS

It is assumed that you are familiar with the general principles of the four-stroke engine and understand the purpose of the controls which operate the engine and gearbox. Before starting up and attempting to ride your Royal Enfield it is advisable, if you are a novice, to sit on the dualseat and familiarize yourself with the disposition and movement of the various levers, pedals, and switches. Also consider the effect of operating each control while the engine is running and while riding.

The Control Layout. The control layout shown in Fig. 3 applies to all 1948–66 250 c.c. and all 1963–5 350 c.c. models. The controls may conveniently be divided into three groups: (1) the engine controls, (2) the motor-cycle controls, and (3) the electrical controls. An ammeter to show whether the battery is being charged, and a speedometer to indicate road speed and mileage, are mounted together with the lighting switch just in front of the handlebars. Note the following points—

The Handlebar Controls. The throttle twist-grip, the air lever, the front brake lever, and the clutch lever are all operated by *inward* movement.

The Throttle Twist-grip. This controls engine speed and has a full movement of about one-quarter of a complete turn. With the twist-grip fully closed the throttle slide in the carburettor does not close completely if the carburettor throttle stop is set to give a good tick-over when idling in traffic and after starting up.

When starting a Royal Enfield from cold it is important to use only a very small throttle opening (about one-eighth of the total twist-grip movement), otherwise it may not be possible to effect a quick start.

The Air Lever. The air lever (which enables the ratio of air and petrol to be varied) must be closed completely for starting from cold, or one-third to one-half opened when starting from warm. At all other times keep the air lever wide open. Occasionally it may be found desirable to keep the air lever only three-quarters open until the engine reaches its normal running temperature when the air lever should be fully opened.

The Ignition Switch. The purpose of the ignition switch is to enable the engine to be stopped by switching off the ignition, no exhaust-valve lifter being provided as is the case with many large capacity four-stroke motor-cycles. The ignition switch is located on the near-side toolbox cover and is actuated by a key.

On the 1965 and later "Continental G.T." model the ignition switch is enclosed (together with the coil and rectifier) in a fibre-glass cover above the battery. This cover can readily be sprung off or on from its three securing screws.

The ignition is switched off when the key is in the *vertical* position and the ignition must always be left switched off when the machine is not being ridden. Turn the key *clockwise* to the "IGN" position to switch on the ignition for starting and normal running. Should the battery become

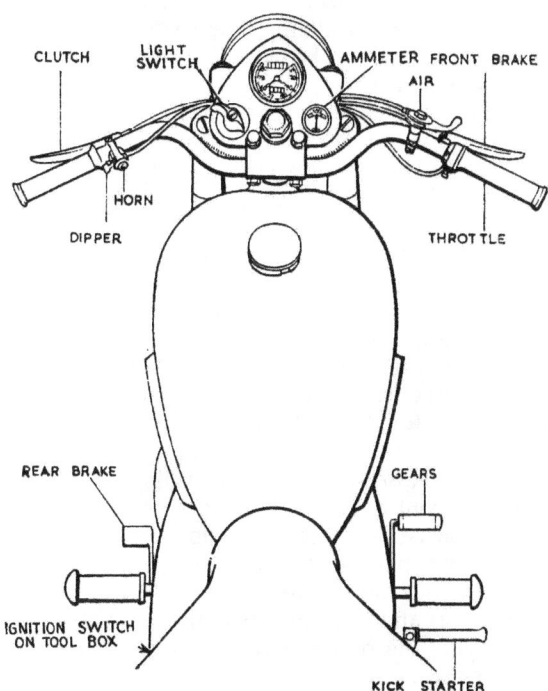

Fig. 3. The Control Layout on all 250 and 350 c.c. Models
(*The Enfield Cycle Co. Ltd.*)

discharged the engine can be started by turning the ignition key *anti-clockwise* to the "EMG" position to obtain emergency ignition. Once the engine has started the ignition switch key must be moved *clockwise* right across to the normal starting position. This is important. On later Royal Enfields it is necessary to push the key in before turning it anti-clockwise.

The Lighting Switch. The lighting switch has the following three positions—

"OFF"—No lights on, and speedometer light switched off.

"L"—Headlamp pilot bulb, tail lamp, and speedometer light switched on.

"H"—Headlamp main bulb, tail lamp, and speedometer light switched on.

For all normal riding by night the lighting switch should be kept in the "H" position. The "L" position should be used for parking for short periods and when riding in brightly lit streets.

The Dipper Switch. This determines whether the headlamp double-filament main bulb gives a horizontal or dipped beam. To prevent dazzle it is courteous to dip the headlamp beam when passing an oncoming vehicle on a dimly lit road. The extensive use of the dipper switch in towns is also recommended.

The Clutch Lever. The clutch lever (which disconnects and re-connects the drive from the engine to the rear wheel) should always be used *progressively and fully* when starting and stopping the machine and during each gear change. Never use the clutch for reducing speed or coasting down hills.

The Foot Gear-change Pedal. The foot gear-change pedal on the off-side (see Fig. 4) enables four or five (on the 1962-3 "Crusader Super 5") gear ratios and "neutral" to be obtained. "Neutral" lies between first and second gears. All upward gear changes are made by *downward* movement of the pedal with the toe, and all changes down by *upward* movement. The gear-change pedal always returns to the same position after each gear change is made, ready for the next gear change. A small pointer on the outside of the crankcase off-side cover (*see* Fig. 4) indicates which gear is engaged, but never look down at this while riding.

The Brakes. The front-brake lever on the handlebars and the rear-brake pedal close to the near-side footrest should be used *simultaneously* and not separately. Note that Royal Enfield brakes are normally powerful and that the use of undue hand or foot pressure besides being unnecessary, is harmful to the tyres and transmission. It is advisable to throttle right down before applying the brakes and also in many instances to change down into a lower gear.

Is the Riding Position Good? A comfortable riding position is essential. Note that you can alter the positions of the handlebars, footrests, and all controls (including the rear-brake pedal and the gear-change lever). Set all controls to suit your physical requirements and see that you are really comfortable on the machine.

STARTING THE ENGINE

Before Starting Up. First be sure that there is a sufficient quantity of engine oil of the correct type and grade in the oil tank and gearbox, both of which are integral with the crankcase (*see* Fig. 4). For instructions on engine and gearbox replenishment, see Chapter III. If a lengthy run is contemplated, check that there is sufficient petrol in the tank which has a capacity of $3\frac{1}{2}$ gal., and also check that the tyre pressures are correct (*see* page 101).

HANDLING YOUR MOUNT

On Royal Enfield machines the petrol and oil tank filler caps are opened by turning the cap *anti-clockwise* until the catch is felt, pushing the cap down, and then turning it *anti-clockwise* as far as possible, and lifting the cap off. To tighten a cap, push it down and then turn *clockwise* to the maximum extent.

Starting Procedure. To start up the engine use the following procedure—

1. Turn on the petrol by pushing in the hexagonal button. A small lever on earlier models is located above the petrol tap. By turning this lever *clockwise* a reserve supply of petrol is retained in the tank. To draw on the reserve supply turn the lever *anti-clockwise*. Later type Royal Enfields have a tap which turns down against its stop in the "ON" position and vice versa. On these later machines a reserve supply of petrol cannot be retained. The 1963-5 "Continental" and the 1965-6 "Continental G.T." models have a racing type quick-release filler operated by a small trigger lever at the rear.

2. Check that the foot gear-change pedal is in the "neutral" position. Verify by means of the small pointer on the outside of the crankcase off-side cover (*see* Fig. 4) or by noting whether the rear wheel can be spun round.

3. Switch on the ignition by turning the ignition key *clockwise*. Turn it *anti-clockwise* for emergency ignition if the battery is discharged.

4. Open the throttle very slightly by turning the twist-grip inwards about *one-eighth* of its total movement.

5. Close the air lever completely unless the engine is warm. In this case open the air lever about one-third to one-half. The best position is obtained by practical experience.

6. If the engine is quite cold, momentarily depress the tickler on the carburettor float-chamber, but do not flood the carburettor so that petrol begins to drip from it. If the engine is warm do not depress the tickler, otherwise the mixture may become excessively rich.

7. Rotate the engine sharply by applying a long swinging kick on the kick-starter pedal. The engine should fire immediately. If the engine fails to fire at the first or second attempt, try kicking the engine over with a slightly greater throttle opening. The best setting is soon obtained from practical experience and varies slightly with different engines.

Should you experience any difficulty in kicking the engine over, engage a gear and gently wheel the machine backwards a few inches until engine compression is felt. Then engage "neutral" and apply a long swinging kick to the kick-starter pedal.

8. When the engine starts up, progressively open the air lever until it is wide open. Set the throttle opening to give a moderately fast tick-over. Do not allow the engine to run slowly or to race, and do not continue to run the engine with the machine stationary for more than a few minutes. Also keep the doors of a garage wide open to prevent carbon monoxide fumes accumulating.

GEAR CHANGING

Moving Off. If you are a novice learn to ride on a quiet road and keep away from heavy traffic until you learn to handle your mount well and have acquired confidence. It is assumed that you have attended to all

Fig. 4. Off-side View of the "Crusader" Type Power Unit with the Gearbox and Oil Tank Integral with the Crankcase

Externally, all 250, 350 c.c. 1958–66 power units are similar but on the earlier "Crusader 250" and the "250 Clipper" a cast-iron instead of an aluminium-alloy cylinder head is fitted. Internally, various engines vary in respect of cubic capacity, compression and gear ratios, carburettor settings, overhead-rocker bearings, and crankshaft design

1. Felt oil filter
2. Oil-tank filler cap
3. Gearbox filler-plug
4. Gearbox oil-level screw
5. Gear indicator
6. Foot gear-change pedal
7. Grease nipple for foot gear-change
8. Clutch-cable adjuster
9. Main clutch-adjuster
10. Contact-breaker cover
11. Rectifier
12. Ignition coil in tool-box

(*By courtesy of* "*Motor Cycle*")

legal preliminaries and have read and understand the Highway Code, or most of it. Then ease the machine off its stand with the engine running and "neutral" engaged. While astride the dualseat, fully disengage the clutch and engage first gear. Raise the foot gear-change pedal to its full extent with the toe and then release the pedal. If the gear does not readily engage, move the machine slightly backwards or forwards while using the gear control, until gear engagement is felt.

Now move off. Gradually open the throttle by turning the twist-grip inwards and simultaneously engage the clutch by releasing the clutch lever on the handlebars. As the clutch plates engage, the machine will begin to move forward and gain momentum. As the engine takes up the load its speed tends to fall and this tendency must be countered by progressively opening the throttle. A smooth take-off without jerk or transmission snatch is soon mastered and correct coordination of the controls becomes instinctive.

Changing Up. When the speedometer indicates about 12 m.p.h. disengage the clutch and simultaneously close the throttle slightly. Pause a second and then engage second gear by *depressing* the foot gear-change pedal with the toe to its *full extent* and then releasing it. A firm and decisive movement should be made, but do not use force on the pedal. This is liable to damage the selector mechanism. As soon as you engage second gear gradually re-engage the clutch and again open the throttle to take up the load and increase the speed of the machine. When a speed of about 20 m.p.h. is reached engage third gear, using the same procedure as for second gear. Finally when a speed of about 30 m.p.h. is reached engage fourth or top gear. Top gear on "Continental" models is, of course, fifth gear. Five gears are also provided as an optional extra on "Crusader Sports" models. With a five-speed gearbox suitable change-up road speeds are 12, 17, 28, and 35 m.p.h. The previously mentioned road speeds for gear changing are intended only as a rough guide and the optimum road speeds depend on whether the road is level or not. When commencing to climb a steep hill somewhat higher road speeds are desirable in the intermediate gears. Excessive speeds must, however, always be avoided.

Gear changes should be made smoothly and silently and fierce acceleration, which is unkind to the tyres and transmission, should be avoided. As soon as you are cruising comfortably in top gear, keep the air lever fully open, controlling road speed by means of the throttle only. It is most important never to allow the engine to knock or "pink" and when accelerating or hill climbing it may be necessary, especially if the engine has not warmed up thoroughly, to close the air lever slightly for a brief period.

Changing Down. Change down when your road speed drops considerably because of road, traffic, or wind conditions. On no account allow your engine to "slog" with a high gear engaged. When changing down, the control movements should be made slightly quicker than when changing up, and each gear change should be made deliberately and firmly. Always avoid using excessive pressure on the foot gear-change pedal.

On a model with a four-speed gearbox when traffic, road or other conditions reduce your road speed (with top gear engaged) to approximately

25 m.p.h., change down into third gear. When your road speed falls to about 12 m.p.h., change down into second gear. Change down into first gear at about 6 m.p.h. These gear changing figures are, of course, only approximate.

Make each downward gear change by smartly and simultaneously disengaging the clutch, opening the throttle momentarily, and *raising* the foot gear-change pedal to its *full extent*. The toe must, of course, be positioned under the gear-change pedal. As when making upward gear changes, you can feel when a gear engages properly, and the gear-change pedal automatically returns to its previous position after each change is made and the foot is removed. After making each downward gear change, adjust the throttle opening to prevent the engine running too fast. The speed of engine rotation automatically increases relative to the speed of the motor-cycle as each downward gear change is made, thus calling for a reduced throttle opening.

To change down into first (bottom) gear it is not *essential* to complete the full gear changing procedure for each intermediate gear, although this should be done when hill climbing. An experienced rider can rapidly change down into first gear by slowing down to a crawl, disengaging the clutch and making two or three full upward movements of the gear-change pedal in quick succession, according to whether third or fourth gear was previously engaged. Each time he raises the gear-change pedal he "blips" the engine by opening the throttle slightly. The clutch is then gently re-engaged. This method of changing down is not recommended for novices.

Climbing Hills. Never allow your engine to labour on a hill and never try to force an unwilling mount up a steep hill with a high gear engaged. Hill climbing requires a good power output and thus the engine revolutions must be kept reasonably high. Always make full use of the Royal Enfield gearbox and change down *in good time*. If a tendency for "pinking" occurs, close the air lever slightly, but only for a brief period.

Just prior to climbing a hill it is desirable to increase the speed and momentum of the machine by giving it plenty of throttle, but this does not apply to a machine which has not been properly run-in. Change down to a lower gear while the machine has plenty of momentum. A fast climb is possible if a change down is made in good time and further changes down higher up the gradient may then be unnecessary. Your Royal Enfield should romp up all moderate gradients and only one gear change should be required.

When descending steep hills, open the air lever wide and close the throttle. This will not only cool the engine but it will enable engine compression to act as a powerful brake.

To Stop the Machine. Apply the front and rear brakes simultaneously, change down into first gear, and disengage the clutch before the motor-cycle comes to rest. The engine may be kept running with the clutch disengaged if the stop is only brief, but change down into "neutral" if the engine is kept running for any length of time. To engage "neutral" from first gear *slightly and very gently depress* the foot gear-change pedal with the clutch disengaged. Do not depress the pedal to its full extent, otherwise you will miss "neutral" and engage second gear. A light touch is necessary, and be careful to re-engage the clutch gradually in case second gear is engaged.

To Stop the Engine. Close the throttle and switch off the ignition by turning the ignition key to the *vertical* position. When you park or garage your mount, always leave the ignition switched off and remove the ignition key. Note that it is advisable to close the petrol tap when you leave your machine standing with the engine stopped for more than a few minutes. If petrol runs through the induction system from a flooding carburettor oil dilution may occur and cause excessive engine wear.

RUNNING-IN

Proper Running-in is Vital. If you own a brand new Royal Enfield or a second-hand mount with a reconditioned engine, you must run-in the engine most carefully for about the first 500 miles. You will then obtain the maximum life from your engine and progressively improve its performance. Neglect to run-in the engine carefully may *permanently* spoil its efficiency. Piston temperature is the vital factor and this depends not only on speed and throttle opening, but also on how long a rather fast speed and wide throttle opening have been maintained.

Bearing surfaces when new appear to be dead smooth, but actually they are covered with fine tool marks (*see* Fig. 5) which are invisible to the naked eye. Until these tool marks disappear and a mirror-like gloss and hardness spread all over, local friction is liable to occur and the oil film may break down at one or more vital places.

Proper running-in involves *progressively* increasing the load on the engine and keeping the engine as cool as possible by avoiding excessive piston speed and throttle openings.

To reduce the risk of piston seizure during the vital running-in period the Royal Enfield machines have a piston which is formed slightly oval, but this ovality in no way minimizes the essential need for careful running-in. Note the following points—

1. Pay due regard to correct lubrication of the engine, gearbox and machine. After riding 500 miles drain the oil from the oil tank (integral with the crankcase) and engine sump. Also clean the felt oil filter, and also the gauze filter fitted in the timing case of the 1962-3 "Crusader Super 5" and all later models. The appropriate lubrication instructions are given in Chapter III.

2. Do not permit the engine to tick-over for more than a few minutes with the motor-cycle stationary.

3. Make the engine run as light as possible by making full use of the

four- or five-speed gearbox, but do not allow the engine to run too fast in the lower gears. Keep its heat down.

4. Never allow the engine to labour by running too slowly in top gear or through neglecting to change down to a lower gear in good time when hill climbing. After climbing a steep hill, allow the engine to cool on the other side (*see* page 10).

5. After covering several hundred miles check the valve clearances, the contact-breaker gap, and the adjustment of the brakes, secondary chain

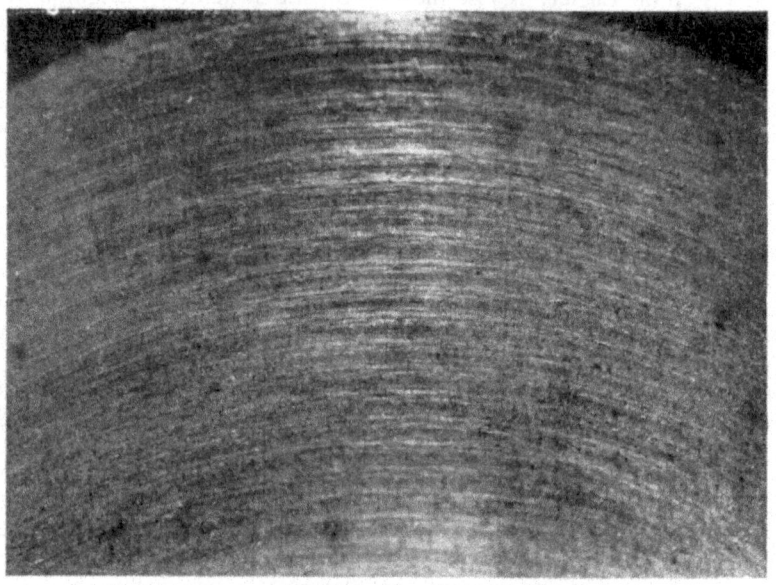

FIG. 5. BEFORE RUNNING-IN THE APPARENTLY SMOOTH CYLINDER BORE SURFACE LOOKS LIKE THIS UNDER A LENS

During careful running-in the numerous tool marks shown gradually disappear and a mirror-like gloss spreads over the surface of the bore traversed by the piston

and clutch. Some initial bedding-down often occurs. Also check the various external bolts and nuts for tightness.

6. Do not ride at a speed exceeding about 30 m.p.h. during the first 200 miles.

7. Until at least 500 miles have been covered avoid using more than *half throttle*, except for very brief periods.

8. After covering 500 miles it is advisable to facilitate the bedding-down of the piston thrust faces by undertaking short bursts of speed. Gradually increase the duration of these speed bursts until the machine will stand large throttle openings for long periods, but avoid using full throttle on the level or uphill until you have ridden about 1,000 miles.

If Piston Seizure Occurs. If, during running-in, the engine is run for an excessive period with the throttle widely opened a tendency for piston seizure may occur; this is indicated by the engine beginning to slow up. In this event immediately declutch, close the throttle, and allow the engine to cool down for several minutes. If this is done it is unlikely that actual piston seizure will occur, and the piston after cooling will usually free itself automatically.

If an actual piston seizure does occur, remove the piston and have it closely examined by a competent mechanic. It may be necessary for him to ease down some high spots and to eradicate slight smearing of the piston in the vicinity of the piston-ring lands.

During Running-in. It is beneficial to mix Acheson's Colloidal Graphite with the *engine oil* in the proportions of *one pint* per gallon of oil. This protects the bearing surfaces from metal pick-up and makes for cooler running. The valves are also benefited. The compound is obtainable from most garages.

ADVICE ON SAFETY

General Advice on Riding. The number of accidents which occur each year on the roads of Great Britain have now reached disgraceful proportions, and many suffer for years through serious injuries sustained. Motor-cyclists are more prone than car drivers to suffer serious injuries. Always ride with proper consideration for other road users and conform with the law in letter and spirit. There are few disasters on the roads which can truly be called *accidents*. Most are caused by selfishness, carelessness, or sheer recklessness by road users. The author offers the following advice—

1. As mentioned at the beginning of this chapter, *always* wear a crash helmet while riding. A fractured skull and severe concussion, with perhaps internal haemorrhage, can cause a shocking "hangover" for a long period, even years, and can easily prove fatal. Remember that you can buy a crash helmet over the counter, but you cannot buy new brains!

2. Do not become over confident and regularly ride at full throttle on major roads and motorways.

3. Avoid excessive speed on what *appear* to be major roads. These often have minor cross-roads where it is easy to be rammed at right angles.

4. Avoid making excessive noise in built-up areas, especially near hospitals.

5. Ride in a state of constantly expecting the unexpected.

6. Exercise special care at cross-roads, roundabouts, and pedestrian crossings. Be courteous to elderly (often "difficult") and blind pedestrians.

7. Always give *clear* hand signals *in good time*.

8. Keep a safe distance behind all cars and lorries.

9. Never ride fast in foggy conditions. Patches of thick fog may be unexpectedly encountered and can be most dangerous.

10. Apply the brakes very carefully on wet and icy roads.

11. Do not cut-in or indulge in "stunt" riding. Such practices usually terminate in a hospital ward or a mortuary.

12. When travelling fast, especially on motorways, always keep *at a safe distance* behind other vehicles.

13. Besides being kind to other road users, always be kind to your machine.

14. Let your motto be "live and let live."

CHAPTER II

THE AMAL CARBURETTOR

AN Amal "monobloc" type carburettor is secured by two nuts and studs to the inlet port of the cylinder head on all 250 and 350 c.c. engines. It is a most reliable instrument and requires little maintenance. The carburettor settings recommended by the Enfield Cycle Co. Ltd. and provided on all new machines should not normally be interfered with. The settings (*see* page 24) have been carefully chosen to provide good all-round performance and low petrol consumption. Do not attempt to save petrol by fitting a smaller size main jet.

It may be necessary occasionally to make a slow-running adjustment to ensure that the engine ticks-over correctly when the throttle is closed. This adjustment (*see* page 19) is quite simple. It is desirable about every 5,000 miles to remove any foreign matter collected in the carburettor float chamber or main-jet cover nut. After completing a very considerable mileage remove, dismantle, inspect and thoroughly clean the entire carburettor. The "monobloc" carburettor can be readily dismantled and reassembled. An exploded view of the instrument is shown on page 22. It has only two controls: the air lever and the throttle twist-grip. Their use is referred to on page 4. Two adjuster screws are provided on top of the carburettor mixing chamber for taking up slack in the two control cables.

"MONOBLOC" CARBURETTOR DETAILS

The Pilot Air-adjusting Screw. This adjusting screw, shown at (*29*) in Fig. 6, regulates the suction imposed on the pilot jet, shown at (*9*) in Fig. 7, by controlling the volume of air which mixes with the petrol. It controls the mixture strength for idling and also for initial throttle openings (up to one-eighth throttle).

The Throttle Stop. The throttle-stop screw, shown at (*30*) in Fig. 6, is normally adjusted to prop the throttle valve open sufficiently to enable the engine to tick-over nicely when the throttle twist-grip is fully closed. To obtain good slow running a combined adjustment of the throttle-stop screw and the pilot air-adjusting screw is required.

The Main Jet. This jet, shown at (*13*) in Fig. 7, controls the fuel supply at throttle openings exceeding three-quarters open. At smaller throttle openings the fuel supplied passes through the main jet, but the amount is decreased owing to the needle in the needle-jet, shown at (*15*) in Fig. 7, having a controlling effect. The main jet is screwed into the needle-jet and can readily be withdrawn after removing the main-jet cover nut shown at (*12*) in Fig. 7.

Each Amal main jet is numbered and calibrated so that its precise discharge is known. Thus it follows that any two main jets having the same number are identical in all respects. The larger the jet, the higher is its

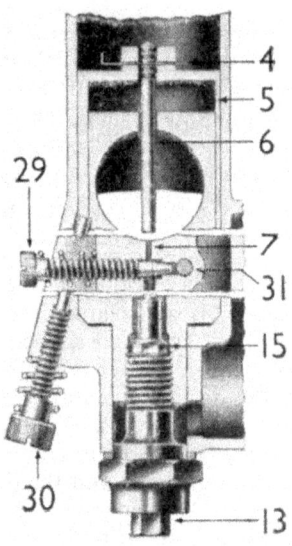

Fig. 6. Showing the Throttle-stop and Pilot Air-adjusting Screw for Slow-running Adjustment

For key to numbered parts, *see* page 17

number. It is not advisable to use a main jet larger than the size recommended by The Enfield Cycle Co. Ltd.

The Jet-needle and Needle-jet. The jet-needle, shown at (*6*) in Fig. 6, is attached to, and moves with, the throttle valve. Being tapered, it permits more or less fuel to pass through the needle-jet, shown at (*15*) in Fig. 7, as the throttle is opened or closed respectively. This applies throughout the range of throttle openings, except at full throttle and when idling. The needle-jet is of a specified size, and normally its size should not be changed except when using alcohol fuels for racing.

As may be seen in Fig. 6, the position of the jet-needle (*6*) relative to the throttle opening can be adjusted according to the mixture required by securing the needle to the throttle valve with the needle spring-clip (*4*) in a particular groove, five of which are provided. Position 3, for example, means the *third groove from the top*. At throttle openings from one-quarter to three-quarters open *raising* the needle *enriches* the mixture,

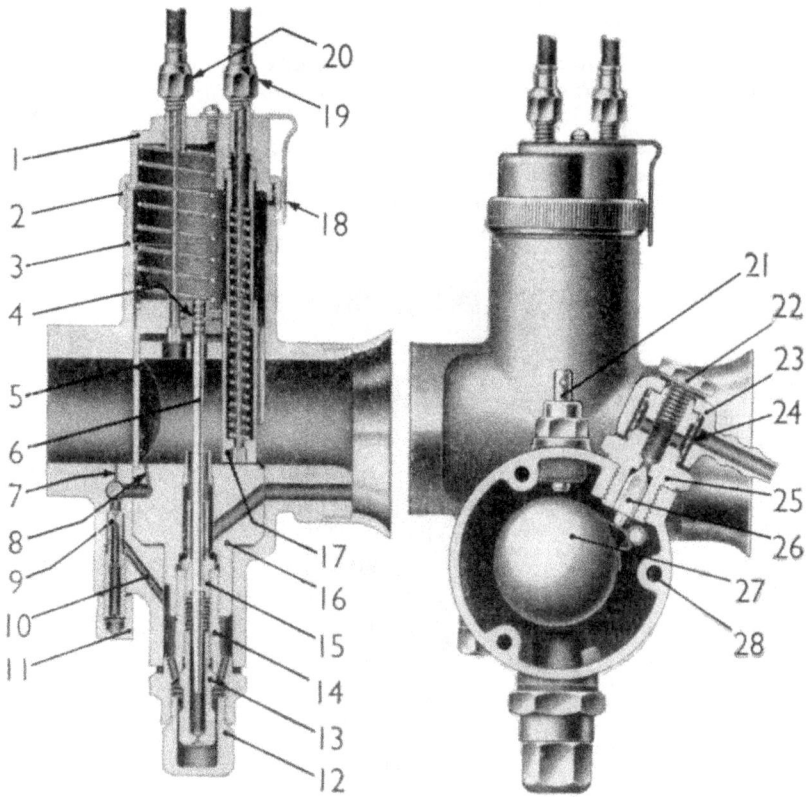

FIGS. 7 AND 8. SECTIONAL VIEWS THROUGH (LEFT) THE MIXING CHAMBER AND (RIGHT) THE FLOAT CHAMBER OF AMAL "MONOBLOC" CARBURETTOR

Key to Figs. 6–11

1. Mixing-chamber cap
2. Mixing-chamber lock-ring
3. Mixing chamber
4. Jet-needle clip
5. Throttle valve
6. Jet-needle (tapered)
7. Pilot outlet
8. Pilot by-pass
9. Pilot jet (detachable)
10. Feed to pilot jet
11. Pilot-jet cover nut
12. Main-jet cover nut
13. Main jet
14. Main-jet holder
15. Needle-jet
16. Jet block
17. Air valve
18. Locking spring for *2*
19. Cable adjuster (air)
20. Cable adjuster (throttle)

21. Tickler
22. Banjo bolt
23. Banjo
24. Nylon filter
25. Needle seating
26. Float-chamber needle
27. Float (hinged)
28. Float-chamber cover screws
29. Pilot air-adjusting screw
30. Throttle-stop screw
31. Air passage to pilot jet
32. Feed holes in *9*
33. "Bleed" holes in *15*
34. Primary air-choke
35. Primary air-passage
36. Throttle-valve cut-away
37. Float chamber
38. Float-chamber cover
39. Locating screw for *16*
40. Jet block fibre seal

while *lowering* the needle *weakens* it. The needle itself is made in one size only, and its position should not normally be changed.

How the Instrument Works. The "monobloc" instrument includes: a horizontal float-chamber made integral with the carburettor body; a float needle of moulded nylon; a top petrol feed; a needle-jet with "bleed" holes giving two-way compensation; and a detachable pilot jet which can be

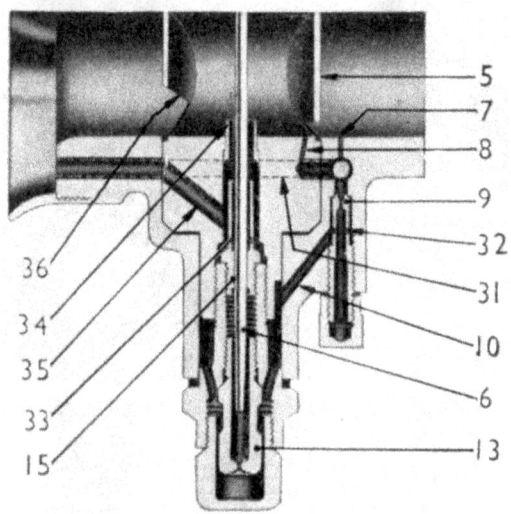

FIG. 9. DIAGRAMMATIC SECTION THROUGH PART OF AMAL "MONOBLOC" CARBURETTOR

This shows only the lower half of the throttle chamber and the internal primary air passage to the main jet and pilot system. The throttle valve is shown slightly open. For key to numbered parts *see* page 17

easily cleaned. Details of the carburettor are shown in Figs. 6–11 and the accompanying key indicates *all* the numbered parts.

Referring to Figs. 7–9, the hinged float (*27*) maintains a constant level of petrol in the needle-jet (*15*) and the pilot jet (*9*), and it cuts off the petrol supply when the engine stops.

The selection of the appropriate jet sizes and main choke bore ensures the proper atomizing and proportioning of the petrol and air sucked into the engine. The air valve (*17*) is normally kept fully raised and the throttle valve (*5*), controlled by the handlebar twist-grip, controls the volume of mixture and therefore the power; at all throttle openings a correct mixture is automatically obtained. The carburettor operates in four stages.

When opening the throttle from the fully closed position to one-eighth open (for idling) the mixture is supplied by the pilot jet (*9*), and mixture strength is determined by the setting of the knurled pilot air-adjusting screw shown at (*29*) in Fig. 6. As the throttle is opened farther the main-jet system comes into action, the mixture being augmented from the main jet (*13*) via the pilot by-pass (*8*) shown in Fig. 7.

The amount of cut-away on the atmospheric side of the throttle valve regulates the petrol-air ratio between one-eighth and one-quarter throttle. The needle-jet (*15*) and the jet-needle (*6*) take over mixture regulation between one-quarter and three-quarter throttle, and mixture strength is determined by the vertical position of the jet-needle (*6*) attached to the throttle valve (*5*). When the throttle is opened beyond three-quarter, the mixture strength is determined by the size of the main jet (*13*).

Note that the main jet does not spray petrol direct into the carburettor mixing chamber, but petrol discharges through the needle-jet (*15*) into the primary air chamber. From there it enters the main choke through the primary air-choke (*34*). The latter has a compensating action in conjunction with "bleed" holes (*33*) in the needle-jet (*15*), which serve the dual purpose of air compensating the mixture from the needle-jet and allowing the fuel to form a well outside and around the needle-jet. This is always available for snap acceleration. Pilot-jet and main-jet behaviour are not affected by this two-way compensation which governs only acceleration at normal cruising speed.

ADJUSTMENT AND FAULTS

Altering Slow-running Adjustment. The adjustment should be made with the engine already *warmed up*. If slow running is poor, screw home the pilot air-adjusting screw and then unscrew it (usually about *two* complete turns) until the engine idles at an excessive speed, with the throttle twist-grip closed and the throttle valve abutting the throttle-stop screw. The air lever should be fully open.

Referring to Fig. 6, unscrew the throttle-stop screw (*30*) until the engine slows up and begins to falter. Then screw the pilot air-adjusting screw (*29*) in or out as required to enable the engine to run regularly and faster. To *weaken* the mixture, screw the pilot air-adjusting screw *outwards*.

Slowly lower the throttle-stop screw until the engine again commences to falter. Then re-set the pilot air-adjusting screw to obtain the best slow running. If after making this second adjustment the engine ticks-over too fast, repeat the adjustment a third time. The combined adjustment sounds complicated, but in practice it is quite simple. It is important to avoid excessive richness of the slow-running mixture, especially if much riding is done on small throttle openings. If the mixture is too rich, considerable running on the pilot jet will occur while riding, with consequently a high fuel consumption.

Aim at obtaining the best tick-over at a *moderate speed* with a mixture bordering on the weak side. The engine should be on the point of "spitting-back." Too slow a tick-over is not recommended as this can cause insufficient lubrication of the cylinder bore while the engine is hot.

An excessively fast tick-over speed should also be avoided as this causes overheating and excessive noise.

Persistent Poor Slow Running. If poor slow running continues after making a careful slow-running adjustment as previously described, the cause may be one or more of the following—
1. An obstructed pilot jet.
2. Air leaks caused through a poor joint between the carburettor flange and cylinder head face.
3. Air leaks due to a worn inlet-valve guide.
4. Weakening of the mixture due to badly seating valves.
5. A sparking plug which has become dirty or oily or has an incorrect gap between the points.
6. An incorrect contact-breaker gap.
7. Incorrect ignition timing.

To Clear an Obstructed Pilot Jet. The pilot jet has a very narrow fuel passage and can easily become choked. Referring to Fig. 10, to remove the pilot jet (*9*), remove its cover nut (*11*) and then unscrew the jet itself. Clean it thoroughly and then blow through it, using the motor-cycle pump. It is also important to see that the air passage to the pilot jet shown at (*31*) in Fig. 9 is unobstructed. This should also be blown through. The same applies to the pilot outlet and pilot by-pass passages shown at (*7*) and (*8*) respectively in Fig. 7.

An Abnormally High Petrol Consumption. Sometimes petrol consumption remains high in spite of the carburettor being carefully tuned for slow running. There are many possible causes. Some are: leakage from the carburettor due to sticking of the moulded-nylon float needle; a faulty float; a poor float-chamber cover joint; a slack main-jet holder or main-jet cover nut; a loose pilot jet; a worn needle-jet; slack petrol pipe union nuts; poor engine compression caused by badly fitting piston rings or pitted valves; binding of the brake shoes on the brake drums; an excessively tight or dry secondary chain; or a slipping clutch. A careful investigation for the cause must be made.

Some less obvious reasons for a high petrol consumption are: running with incorrect valve clearances or weak valve springs; air leaks due to a poor joint between the carburettor flange and inlet-port face; a worn inlet valve guide; or late ignition timing.

Do not attempt to reduce petrol consumption by fitting a smaller size main jet. The size of this jet has no effect unless the motor-cycle is being ridden with the throttle more than half open. Where the reason for a high petrol consumption is found difficult or impossible to detect, try lowering the tapered jet-needle attached to the throttle valve *one notch*. See that the jet-needle clip beds home properly in the needle groove.

THE AMAL CARBURETTOR

CARBURETTOR MAINTENANCE

Dismantling "Monobloc" Carburettor. First see that the petrol tap is closed and disconnect the petrol pipe from the float-chamber union by unscrewing the union nut. Referring to Fig. 10, remove both nuts which secure the carburettor flange to the inlet-port face and unscrew the knurled lock-ring (2) on top of the mixing chamber (3). Then withdraw the carburettor after disconnecting the air-filter rubber sleeve from the carburettor air-intake, where a filter is fitted. While removing the carburettor pull the air valve (17) and the throttle valve (5) from the mixing chamber and tie them up temporarily out of the way. Unless it is desired to inspect the slides closely it is not necessary to remove them from their cables. Check that the carburettor flange heat-resisting washer is in good condition.

Further dismantling of the carburettor for cleaning and inspection is straightforward. Again referring to Fig. 10, to remove the jet-needle (6), withdraw the jet-needle clip (4) on top of the throttle valve (5) and remove the needle. To obtain access to the float (27) remove the three screws (28) securing the float-chamber cover (38) to the float chamber (37). Lift out the hinged float (27) and withdraw the moulded-nylon needle (26). Lay both aside for cleaning. The float-chamber vent, by the way, is embodied in the tickler assembly (21), and the top-feed union houses a filter element of nylon which is readily accessible for cleaning. To remove the nylon filter (*see* Fig. 11) unscrew the banjo bolt (22), remove the steel washer, the banjo (23), and then the nylon filter (24).

To remove the main jet (13), remove the main-jet cover nut (12) and unscrew the jet from the jet holder (14). Remove the jet block locating-screw (39) to the left of and slightly below the pilot air-adjusting screw (29). Then push or tap out the jet block (16) through the larger end of the mixing chamber body. To remove the pilot jet (9), remove the pilot-jet cover nut (11) and unscrew the jet.

Cleaning the Carburettor. Wash all the carburettor components thoroughly clean with petrol and blow through the various ducts and passages to ensure that they are quite clear. Do not use a fluffy rag for drying purposes. Pay special attention to the small pilot jet passages in the jet block. Be sure to remove all impurities from the inside of the float chamber. Also do not forget to clean the detachable pilot jet and the nylon filter shown at (24) in Fig. 11.

Inspecting the Components. If the carburettor has been in continuous service for a considerable period inspect the various components after dismantling the carburettor. Note the following—
   1. *The Float Chamber.* Check that the vent is unobstructed and that the float is in perfect condition. Clean the moulded-nylon needle very thoroughly, and be careful not to damage it. If it tends to stick in its seating, relieve its three bearing edges with a fine file. The needle seating

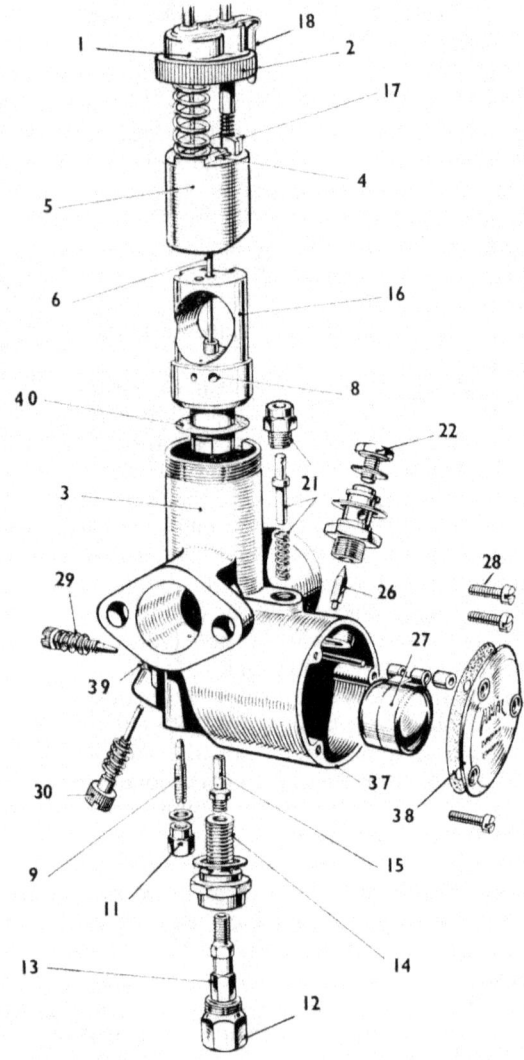

Fig. 10. Exploded View of Amal "Monobloc" Carburettor
A key to the numbered parts of the carburettor is given on page 17. See also Fig. 11

shown at (*25*) in Fig. 11 must be absolutely clean. See that the small nylon filter (*24*) is undamaged and contains no obstructions. Check that the joint faces of the float-chamber cover and the float chamber are not damaged or bruised, and that the joint washer is in sound condition, otherwise some petrol leakage from the cover joint may occur.

2. *The Throttle Valve.* Check that the throttle valve slides in the mixing chamber without excessive play. If excessive play exists, renew the throttle valve immediately.

3. *The Jet-needle Clip.* The spring clip securing the tapered jet-needle to the throttle valve must grip the needle firmly, and free rotation of the needle must not occur, otherwise the needle groove will become worn and necessitate a new needle being fitted. When the carburettor is reassembled be sure to replace the jet-needle with the spring clip in the correct needle groove (*see* page 16).

4. *The Needle-jet.* Inspect its orifice for signs of wear which are generally present after a mileage of about 15,000 miles. The tapered jet-needle is made of hard stainless-steel and its tapered part does not wear.

5. *The Jet Block.* Before tapping this home in the mixing chamber verify by blowing that the pilot-jet ducts are unobstructed and see that the jet block fibre-seal (shown at (*40*) in Fig. 10) is in good condition.

6. *The Carburettor Flange.* Examine this for truth with a straight-edge. Slight distortion sometimes occurs after a considerable mileage, and this may cause an air leak. See that the heat-resisting joint washer is in perfect condition. If it is not, renew it. If the face of the carburettor flange is slightly concave, file the face carefully and then rub the face on emery cloth laid on a surface plate until a straight-edge shows the face surface to be dead flat. Alternatively have the face machined dead flat by using a grinder at a service garage.

To Reassemble "Monobloc" Carburettor. Assemble the carburettor in the reverse order of dismantling. Referring to Fig. 10, screw home the pilot jet (*9*) and the pilot-jet cover nut (*11*), not omitting to replace its washer. Push or tap home the jet block (*16*) and fibre seal (*40*) through the large end of the mixing chamber (*3*). Check that the fibre seal fitted to the stub of the jet block is in sound condition. Then fit the jet block locating-screw (*39*). Screw the main-jet holder (*14*) into the jet block after checking that the washer for the holder is sound and that the needle-jet (*15*) is securely screwed into the top of the holder. Now screw home the main jet (*13*) into the base of the main-jet holder and replace the main-jet cover nut (*12*).

Replace the moulded-nylon needle (*26*) in the float chamber (*37*), and fit the hinged float (*27*) with the *narrow* side of the hinge uppermost. It must contact the nylon needle. Do not omit the short distance collar on the spindle. Afterwards fit the float-chamber cover (*38*) and replace the three securing screws (*28*). Be careful to tighten these three screws evenly. Before replacing the cover it is advisable to renew the washer and make sure that the float chamber and cover joint faces are absolutely clean. Replace items (22)–(24) shown in Fig. 11. Note that the small nylon filter (24) has longitudinal supports moulded in its sides. When replacing the filter see that these supports do not obstruct the feed holes in (25), otherwise some petrol starvation may result. Tighten the banjo bolt (22) securely when the petrol pipe is later connected to the banjo by the union nut.

If previously removed, attach the jet-needle (6) to the throttle valve (5) and secure with the jet-needle clip (4). Make sure that the clip enters the correct groove on the needle (*see* page 25).

Fit the heat-resisting washer to the face of the inlet port. Renew it if not in perfect condition. Some models have a rubber "O" ring. Then

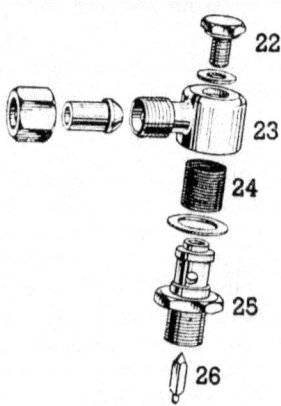

FIG. 11. SHOWING THE NYLON FILTER AND ADJACENT PARTS
For key to numbered parts, *see* page 17
(*The Enfield Cycle Co. Ltd.*)

smear a little oil on the outside of the throttle valve and ease the throttle valve (5) and the air valve (17) down into the mixing chamber (3). When easing the throttle valve home make sure that the tapered jet-needle (6) really enters the hole in the jet block (16). Offer up the carburettor and secure its flange firmly to the cylinder-head face and washer by means of the two nuts. It is important to tighten both nuts the same amount. Tighten down firmly the mixing-chamber knurled lock-ring (2) so as to secure the mixing-chamber cap (1), and see that the throttle valve slides up and down freely when the cap is secured. Finally re-connect the petrol pipe and firmly tighten the union nut and the banjo bolt shown at (22) in Fig. 11. Re-connect the air filter where fitted.

The Correct Amal Carburettor Settings. All new Royal Enfield motor-cycles have the carburettor settings given below and the makers recommend that these settings should not be altered.

THE AMAL CARBURETTOR

1958–62 "Crusader 250" and 1958–65 "250 Clipper." The correct carburettor setting is: main jet: 120, except on the 1964–5 "250 Clipper" which has a main jet size 95; throttle valve: 375/3½; pilot jet: 25; needle-jet: 0·105; needle clip in No. 3 groove.

1959–66 "Crusader Sports." The correct carburettor setting is: main jet: 140, except on the 1964–6 model which has a main jet size 130; throttle valve: 376/3½; pilot jet: 25; needle-jet: 0·106; needle clip in No. 3 groove.

1963–5 "Continental" and 1962–3 "Crusader Super 5." The correct carburettor setting is: main jet: 180, except on the 1964–5 "Continental" which has a main jet size 170; throttle valve: 376/3½; pilot jet: 25; needle-jet: 0·106; needle clip in No. 4 groove.

1963–5 "350 Bullet." The correct carburettor setting is: main jet: 180, except on the 1964–5 model which has a main jet size 160; throttle valve: 376/3½; pilot jet: 25; needle-jet: 0·106; needle clip in No. 3 groove.

1965 250 c.c. "Olympic." The correct carburettor setting is: main jet: 95; throttle valve: 375/3½; pilot jet: 25; needle-jet: 0·106; needle clip in No. 3 groove.

1965–6 "Continental G.T." The correct carburettor setting is: main jet: 260; throttle valve: 389/3½; pilot jet: 30; needle-jet: 0·106; needle clip in No. 3 groove.

THE AIR FILTER

Some Royal Enfields have a Vokes Micro-Vee felt and gauze air-filter fitted in the off-side of the tool-box. Its object is to prevent dust or grit entering the air intake of the carburettor and thereby increasing engine wear. In hot countries an air filter is usually desirable, but it is not so important in Great Britain. Note that if you do not have an air filter provided, and you wish to fit one, you have only to purchase from a Royal Enfield dealer a felt-and-mesh filter element. On all machines provision is made for fitting an element.

Maintenance. Air passes through the Vokes filter element from outside to inside, and therefore dust or grit mainly collects on the *outer* surface of the element. After a considerable mileage, the felt-and-mesh element should be cleaned by brushing and blowing it with compressed air. It is designed to be used in a dry condition and should not be oiled. Access to the filter is readily obtained.

First remove the off-side lid from the tool-box. You can then see the air-filter cover which is secured by one central screw. After removing this screw, press inwards the top left-hand corner of the cover. The cover will then pivot outwards at the bottom and you can remove it completely. To remove the actual filter, hold it by the metal portion and pull to the left. It will then free itself from the rubber sleeve connected to the air intake of the carburettor.

CHAPTER III

CORRECT LUBRICATION

FRICTION between the surfaces of moving parts cannot be eliminated unless regular and proper lubrication is attended to. Friction produces heat and unnecessary wear. This chapter provides all the information you need to ensure correct lubrication of the engine, gearbox, and various parts of

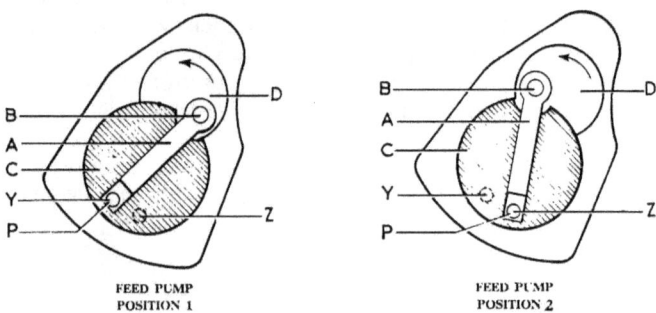

FEED PUMP POSITION 1

FEED PUMP POSITION 2

FIG. 12. DIAGRAM SHOWING ACTION OF OIL-FEED PUMP

Note that the ports in the pump housing are connected as follows: Y: suction from the oil tank; Z: delivery to the big-end bearing. In *feed pump position 1* the plunger A is being drawn out of the back cylinder hole of the disc C by the action of the peg B on the end of the pump spindle D. The port P in the disc C registers with the suction port Y in the housing so that oil is drawn into the cylinder from the oil tank. In *feed pump position 2* the plunger A is being pushed into the cylinder hole in the disc C. The port P in the disc now registers with the delivery port Z in the housing so that oil is forced out of the cylinder to the filter and thence to the big-end bearing

(*The Enfield Cycle Co. Ltd.*)

your motor-cycle. Not much attention is necessary, but this attention is vital to ensure continuous good performance and trouble-free running.

ENGINE LUBRICATION

There are three main portions of the engine where proper lubrication is vital: (*a*) that portion of the cylinder bore traversed by the piston and piston rings (which reciprocate extremely fast); (*b*) the fairly heavy crankshaft assembly, including the mainshaft bearings, and the connecting-rod big-end and small-end bearings; and (*c*) the timing gear and overhead-valve operating mechanism.

The Royal Enfield Dry-sump System. This is an entirely automatic system and the accompanying diagrams (Figs. 14 and 15) show how the engine oil circulates. The oil tank is made integral with the crankcase. This, besides improving the appearance of the motor-cycle, ensures quick heating of the engine oil in cold weather and complete circulation of the oil as soon as the engine is started.

A duplex-type oil pump is positively driven at half engine speed. It is of the oscillating-disc type and has two pistons. One pumps engine oil under pressure to the big-end bearing and the other returns the oil from the crankcase back to the oil tank and also to the overhead-valve rocker mechanism. To ensure that oil does not collect in the crankcase the return

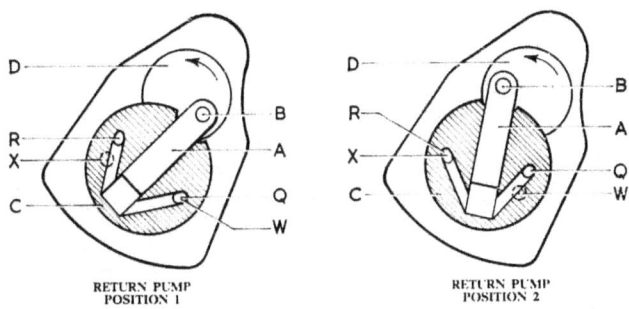

RETURN PUMP
POSITION 1

RETURN PUMP
POSITION 2

FIG. 13. DIAGRAM SHOWING ACTION OF OIL-RETURN PUMP

Note that the ports in the pump housing are connected as follows: *W:* suction from the crankcase; *X:* delivery to the oil tank and overhead rockers. In *return pump position 1* the plunger *A* is being drawn out of the front cylinder-hole in the disc *C* by the action of the peg *B* on the end of the pump spindle *D*. The port *Q* in the disc *C* registers with the suction port *W* in the housing so that oil is drawn into the cylinder from the crankcase sump. In *return position 2* the plunger *A* is being pushed into the cylinder hole in the disc *C*. The port *R* in the disc now registers with the delivery port *X* in the housing so that oil is forced out of the cylinder back to the oil tank and the overhead-rocker gear

(*The Enfield Cycle Co. Ltd.*)

pump piston has double the capacity of the feed pump piston. Both pistons are located in the same disc, but they can be considered as two separate pumps, not being interconnected. The functioning of the pumps is a little difficult for a non-technically minded person to understand but Figs. 12 and 13 explain diagrammatically how the feed and return pumps operate. The arrangement of the pump ports is, of course, a vital factor.

The feed pump sucks engine oil from the oil tank through a pipe in the primary chaincase and forces it through a second pipe to the oil filter and onwards through an internal duct drilled in the primary chaincase to a central hole in the crankshaft. From here the oil passes to the big-end bearing via drilled holes in the crankshaft, assisted by centrifugal action.

Oil splashed off the big-end bearing lubricates the crankshaft main bearings and also the cylinder bore and piston. All surplus oil then collects in the small sump at the bottom of the crankcase rear end. Further lubrication is effected as described in the next two pages.

On Earlier Engines. Referring to Fig. 14, the top of the oil filter is connected to a pressure-control valve which is of the spring-loaded type. This valve is screwed into the top of the crankcase and discharges into the oil tank.

The return pump sucks the oil from the crankcase through a third pipe in the chaincase and delivers it through a fourth pipe to a drilled passage

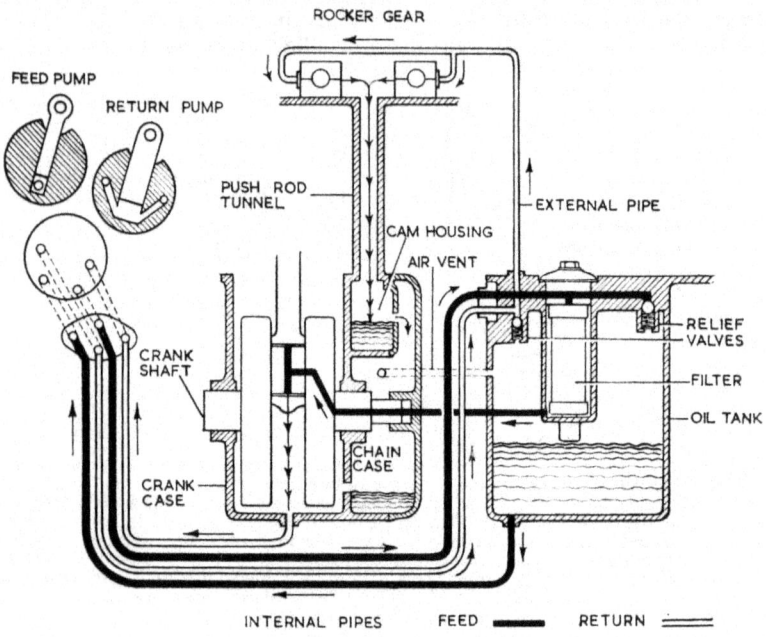

FIG. 14. DIAGRAM SHOWING HOW THE OIL CIRCULATES ON EARLIER ENGINES
(*The Enfield Cycle Co. Ltd.*)

in the top of the crankcase near the oil filter. From the filter most of the engine oil passes through a second valve back to the oil pump, but this valve causes enough back-pressure to force some of the oil in the drilled passage through an external pipe connected to a union on the top of the crankcase to the overhead-rocker bearings on the cylinder head.

The valve stems and push-rods are lubricated by the oil which passes through the overhead-rocker bearings, and oil flows down the push-rod tunnel into the camshaft housing. There the cam followers, the cams, and the gear train driving the contact-breaker and oil pumps are lubricated. The oil level in the camshaft housing is regulated by a hole through which the oil overflows into the primary chaincase, thereby lubricating the primary chain and the timing chain.

The level of oil in the primary chaincase is maintained by another hole between the bottom of the primary chaincase and the crankcase. The oil-return pump picks up all surplus oil which flows back into the crankcase sump.

On Later Engines. Referring to Fig. 15, no relief valve is fitted on top of the crankcase. Oil pressure is controlled entirely by the spring-loaded oil-pump discs.

Engine oil is sucked by the return pump through a third pipe in the primary chaincase and delivered through a fourth pipe to a drilled passage in the top of the crankcase close to the oil filter. From this point most of

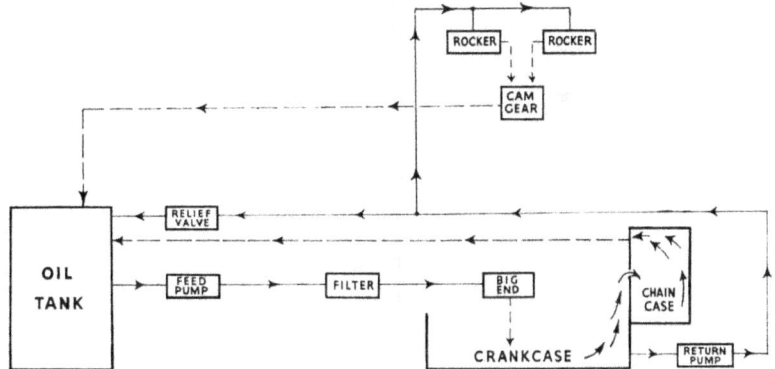

FIG. 15. DIAGRAM SHOWING HOW THE OIL CIRCULATES ON LATER ENGINES
(*The Enfield Cycle Co. Ltd.*)

the oil passes back to the oil tank through a spring-loaded ball valve. The back-pressure created by this valve, however, forces some of the oil in the drilled passage through an external pipe connected to a union on the top of the crankcase to the overhead-rocker bearings.

The push-rods and valve stems are lubricated by the oil which passes through the overhead-rocker bearings. The oil then flows down the push-rod tunnel into the camshaft housing where it lubricates the cam followers, the cams, and the gear train which drives the contact-breaker and oil pumps.

A hole through which the oil overflows into the oil tank controls the oil level in the camshaft housing. Oil from the crankcase passes through the main journal-bearing, and through the pressure-equalizing hole located above the main bearing, and lubricates the primary chain. Surplus oil flung by the chain into a weir located in the top rear portion of the case controls the level of oil in the primary chaincase. The surplus oil drains back into the oil tank through a hole from the weir.

Replenishing the Oil Tank. Remove the filler cap, which is situated just behind the cylinder barrel on the off-side (*see* Fig. 17), and replenish the oil tank regularly about every 200 miles. Should the tank become completely empty, the engine with the dry-sump system of lubrication is entirely starved of oil with, needless to say, disastrous consequences.

Attached to the filler cap is a dipstick and the oil level should be kept well above the bottom of this. *Do not replenish the oil tank above the oil return plug;* this may cause oil to escape past the filler cap. On most engines there are two marks on the dipstick, as indicated in Fig. 16, and

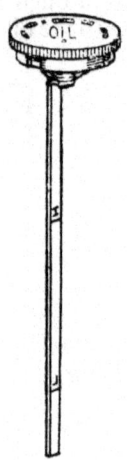

FIG. 16. OIL FILLER CAP WITH DIPSTICK

in this case keep the oil level up to the top mark. Where no mark is provided it is a good plan to file a mark in a suitable position.

Always remember that by keeping a large amount of engine oil in circulation its temperature is kept low and the oil retains its lubricating qualities for a long period. Never run on an inferior type of oil.

Suitable Engine Oils. Always replenish the oil tank with a reputable brand of engine oil of the correct grade. Also buy only from sealed cans or branded cabinets. Suitable engine oils for all 1958 and later 250 c.c. and 350 c.c. engines are as follows—

1. Castrol XXL (Castrolite or XL during winter).
2. Mobiloil AF or BB (A during winter).
3. Shell X-100 40 (X-100 30 during winter).
4. B.P. Energol SAE 40 (Energol SAE 30 during winter).
5. Esso Extra 40/50 (Extra 20W/30 during winter).
6. Regent Havoline 40 (Havoline 30 during winter).

CORRECT LUBRICATION 31

During the running-in period it is beneficial to mix Acheson's Colloidal Graphite with the engine oil (*see* page 13). If this compound is used after running-in is completed, reduce the amount used by *half.*

Multi-grade Oils. Note that some of the manufacturers of the engine oils just mentioned offer special engine lubricants, the viscosity of which is less sensitive than usual to temperature changes. These are classed as SAE 10W/30 or 10W/40 oils and their use will facilitate starting at low temperatures; there may, however, be a slight increase in oil consumption.

Detergent Oils. Some of the oils suitable for Royal Enfield motor-cycles contain detergent additives designed to counteract ring sticking and sludge formation. The degree of detergency varies not only between one make and another but in some cases between different grades of the same make and may even be different for the same grade and make of oil in different parts of the world.

If one of the more highly detergent oils is used in an engine containing large deposits of sludge which have accumulated when running on another grade of oil, this sludge will be loosened and may cause seizure and other trouble due to obstructions in oilways and filters. The following procedure should be adopted when changing to one of the more highly detergent oils, especially if the engine has been used on a normal grade of oil or the oil has not been drained and changed at regular intervals.

1. Drain the engine when the oil is hot and replenish with detergent oil.
2. Run the motor-cycle at a moderate speed for not more than 50 miles.
3. Drain the engine again when the oil is hot, flush out the oil tank with detergent oil, and remove and clean the oil filters. It is desirable to fit a new element in the felt oil filter. Replenish with detergent oil.
4. When the motor-cycle has travelled a further 100 miles check the condition of the filters. If they are found to be clogged, repeat operation 3.

No Adjustment Provided on D.S. System. No adjustment is provided on the dry-sump lubrication system. All parts, including the overhead valve gear, are automatically lubricated with the correct amount of oil. The oil pump has no adjustment. For pump overhaul advice, *see* page 68.

Check the Oil Return Occasionally. It is desirable occasionally to remove the oil tank filler-cap and observe whether oil is flowing satisfactorily through the oil-pressure relief valve. A satisfactory flow shows that the oil pump is working efficiently. An oil pump which fails to function satisfactorily should be immediately dismantled and inspected as described on page 68.

Warming Up the Engine. Some riders run the engine fast immediately after starting up. This is bad practice because until the engine oil reaches a certain temperature it will not circulate with maximum efficiency. Do not allow the engine to tick-over too slowly when warming up because this reduces the speed of oil in circulation, possibly to a dangerous extent when the oil is in a very viscous state. It also induces low-temperature condensation of petrol which is liable to corrode the cylinder bore.

Drain Oil Tank and Engine Sump Every 2,000 Miles. After covering 500 miles and subsequently at regular intervals of about 2,000 miles drain both the oil tank and the engine sump. Place a suitable tray beneath the engine to catch oil as it drains off. To drain the oil tank remove the hexagon-headed plug underneath the near-side of the crankcase. To drain the oil sump remove the small screw on the same side.

To ensure quick and complete draining, drain the oil tank and engine sump after a ride when the oil is warm. If draining is done with the oil cold it is advisable to allow draining to continue overnight. To economize in engine oil it is advisable to drain the oil tank when the level of oil in it is fairly low. After draining of the tank and sump is completed, replace the hexagon-headed plug and small screw, not omitting to replace the two washers. Should you accidentally lose the small screw provided for draining the oil sump, on no account replace it with a *longer* screw as this would be likely to blank off one of the vital internal oil ducts and thereby starve the engine of oil. Tighten the hexagon-headed plug and small screw really firmly and then replenish the oil tank with suitable engine oil (*see* page 30).

Clean the Oil Filter(s) Every 2,000 Miles. On most pre-1963 engines only one filter is provided. This comprises a felt filter of the type shown in Fig. 17. It is connected with the oil supply to the big-end bearing and is positioned in the top of the crankcase on the near-side of the engine just behind the cylinder barrel. On all 1963 and later type engines there is in addition to the felt filter a nylon-gauze filter located inside the timing case (on the near-side) as shown in Fig. 32.

Clean the felt filter, or the felt and the gauze filters, with petrol after covering 500 miles and thereafter regularly every 2,000 miles. It is advisable to renew the element of the felt filter every 5,000 miles. Save the brass ferrule on the bottom end of the old element for fitting to the new element.

To remove the felt filter shown in Fig. 17, unscrew the nut which holds the end cap in position and withdraw the filter element. When re-assembling the felt filter after cleaning, make sure that the spring and spring cup are at the *bottom* end of the filter element, and also check that there is no grit or other foreign matter adhering to the filter element.

To remove the gauze filter shown at (*9*) in Fig. 32, first place a suitable tray beneath the engine to catch escaping oil. Then remove the near-side footrest and withdraw the crankcase near-side cover after removing its 10 securing screws. On a 1963-6 "Continental" model the rev. counter drive is fitted to the crankcase near-side cover and this should be removed by unscrewing the two hexagon-headed screws. Removal of the cover is not affected by the presence of the rev. counter drive, but it is undoubtedly safer and easier to re-mesh the drive *after* replacing the crankcase near-side cover.

Unscrew the filter-cap hexagon and withdraw the gauze element. Do not use a fluffy rag when cleaning it with petrol, and when replacing the gauze element make sure that its blank end faces *towards* the hexagon cap.

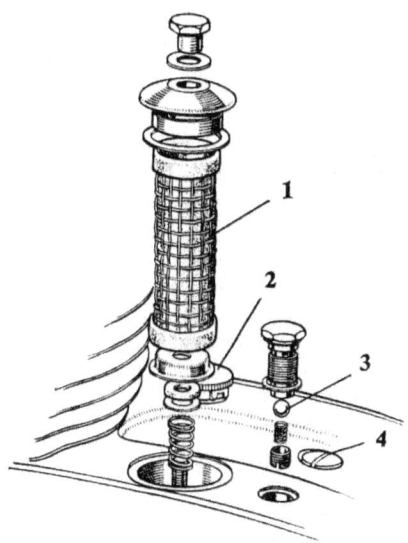

FIG. 17. SHOWING THE FELT OIL FILTER, OIL TANK FILLER-CAP, OIL-PRESSURE RELIEF VALVE, AND GEARBOX FILLER-PLUG

The big-end oil-pressure relief valve shown is omitted on all later type engines
1. The felt element
2. Oil tank filler-cap
3. Ball of big-end oil-pressure relief valve
4. Gearbox filler-plug

(*The Enfield Cycle Co. Ltd.*)

When removing and cleaning the gauze filter also check and if necessary adjust the tension of the timing and primary chains (*see* page 64).

During the replacement of the crankcase near-side cover see that the crankcase and cover faces are clean and apply some jointing compound sparingly. It is advisable to renew the rubber oil-seal bush which is pressed into the cover and fits over the end of the flywheel mainshaft. Smear it with some grease before replacing the cover. Also check that the Neophrene seal and tube which connect with the bottom of the gauze filter are positioned in the recesses in the cover. After replacing the cover and re-meshing the rev. counter drive (where fitted), replenish with about one-third of a pint of engine oil.

Oil-pressure Relief Valves. Except on earlier type Royal Enfields (*see* page 69) the relief valves never require any attention.

The Contact-breaker. About every 3,000 miles remove the small circular cover from the front of the crankcase off-side cover (*see* Fig. 4). This gives access to the Lucas contact-breaker. Smear a little thin oil on the cam, but be most careful not to allow any of it to get on or near the contacts. A dry cam, by the way, sometimes causes a high-pitched squeak. It is advisable also to smear a little thin machine-oil on the automatic ignition-advance mechanism (*see* Fig. 29).

THE MOTOR-CYCLE PARTS

Although engine lubrication is vital, proper lubrication of the motor-cycle parts, especially the gearbox and transmission, should never be neglected. Neglect will spoil the performance of an efficient and well lubricated engine and accelerate wear and tear.

Topping-up the Gearbox. The correct lubricant to use for a four- or five-speed gearbox is *engine oil*, preferably of summer grade (*see* page 30). On no account use any form of grease. Remember that the gear teeth are continually subjected to very high stresses, and therefore the maintenance of engine oil in the gearbox *at the correct level* is extremely important. Top-up the gearbox to the correct level, where found necessary, every 5,000 miles. On a new machine it is advisable to drain and refill the gearbox with fresh oil after covering 1,000 miles, but subsequent draining and refilling should not be necessary more often than once every 5,000 miles. Frequent draining and refilling is quite unnecessary.

To top-up the gearbox remove the filler plug which is located on top of the crankcase (*see* Fig. 17). Also remove the oil-level screw (shown at (*4*) in Fig. 4) from the crankcase off-side cover. Then with a small funnel pour engine oil through the filler-plug orifice until oil begins to exude from the level-screw hole. During replenishment the motor-cycle should be on an even keel. After replenishment replace and firmly tighten the filler plug and the oil-level screw, but do not replace the latter until oil stops running from the level-screw hole.

It is for obvious reasons desirable with a unit-construction engine and gearbox to drain the oil from the gearbox when the engine is warm. Place an oil tray beneath the gearbox and remove the hexagon-headed drain plug located beneath the off-side of the crankcase. After draining the gearbox refill with fresh engine oil of the correct type to the correct level. See that the drain plug is afterwards firmly re-tightened. (*See* page 30 for correct type of oil.)

The Primary Chain. On Royal Enfield engines with unit-construction of the engine and gearbox both the primary chain and the timing chain (*see* Fig. 32) are automatically lubricated and the correct amount of engine oil is constantly maintained in the chaincase by the dry-sump lubrication system.

Should you for any reason remove the crankcase near-side cover, after replacing it remove the inspection cap shown at (*4*) in Fig. 54 and replenish with about *one-third of a pint* of engine oil before starting up the engine, otherwise lubrication of the two chains will not be effected until the dry-sump lubrication system has filled the chaincase to the correct level.

The Secondary Chain. Where a pressed-steel chaincase (*see* Fig. 49) completely encloses the secondary chain, remove the inspection plug from the upper half of the chaincase at frequent intervals and apply engine oil to the chain while rotating the rear wheel with "neutral" engaged. See that the oil from an oil-can is falling upon the bearing surfaces and not merely on the rollers.

Where only a chain-guard is provided, lubricate the exposed secondary chain frequently with graphite grease applied with a brush, or engine oil applied with an oil-can. If engine oil is used, rotate the secondary chain by means of the rear wheel and apply an oil-can to the lower chain run. Remember that if the secondary chain is insufficiently lubricated, undue wear of the chain and the sprockets will occur, and the transmission may become rather harsh.

Every 2,000 miles remove an exposed secondary chain and submerge it in paraffin. If the chain is allowed to soak well, all the dirt will be removed. Hang the chain up to dry and replace it. Before doing this, however, it is a good plan to immerse the chain in a receptacle containing melted grease or tallow. This will penetrate to all the bearing surfaces.

The Steering-head Bearings. These are packed with grease during their initial assembly and no further lubrication is necessary.

The Telescopic Front Forks. No external lubrication is necessary except on 1962–3 "Crusader Super 5" and 1965 "Olympic" models where four grease nipples are provided on the leading-link fulcrum pins. Apply the grease-gun to these nipples about every 500 miles.

On the "Crusader Super 5" and "Olympic" models no internal lubrication maintenance is required; the suspension units are sealed and need no topping-up, but the grease-gun should be applied to four grease nipples, two of which are shown at (*1*) in Fig. 57, every 500 miles. On all other models, however, it may be necessary very occasionally to top-up the damping oil contained in each fork leg. Some leakage past the oil seals does sometimes occur, especially if a motor-cycle is often ridden over rough roads. The onset of sudden damping, giving the effect of "bottoming," indicates that topping-up is needed. When topping-up is necessary use one of the following damping oils—
1. Castrol Castrolite.
2. Shell X-100 20/20W.

3. B.P. Energol SAE 20W.
4. Mobiloil Arctic.
5. Esso Extra 20W/30.
6. Regent Havoline 20/20W.

To top-up each front fork leg where topping-up is provided for and found necessary, use the following procedure. First place your motor-cycle on its central stand to allow both fork legs to extend fully. Then remove the screwed plug from the top of one fork leg, and also the oil-level screw from the rear of the fork tube which slides up and down. Now, using a small funnel, pour in one of the previously-mentioned damping oils until the oil commences to exude from the oil-level screw hole. When oil ceases to flow out, replace the oil-level screw and also the screwed plug. Do not omit the washers. Top-up the other fork leg similarly.

The Grease-gun. An excellent grease-gun is usually supplied in the tool kit. Royal Enfield motor-cycles have few grease nipples requiring routine application of grease with the grease-gun, but such nipples as are provided should not be neglected. Grease canisters intended for filling the grease-gun quickly are available and the use of these canisters obviates the rather messy job of filling the grease-gun by hand. Suitable greases for greasing all motor-cycle parts are—
1. Castrol Castrolease LM.
2. Shell Retinax A.
3. Mobiloil Mobilgrease MP.
4. B.P. Energrease L2.
5. Regent Marfak Multipurpose 2.
6. Esso Multipurpose Grease H.

Wheel Hubs. Every 10,000 miles remove both wheels and repack the hub bearings with one of the above-mentioned greases.

The Speedometer Drive. Every 5,000 miles apply two shots with the grease-gun to the nipple on the speedometer-drive gearbox. About every 10,000 miles remove the inner cable and apply grease sparingly. Feed the cable back into the casing, withdraw about 8 inches, and then wipe off surplus grease.

The Handlebar Controls. Apply the oil-can frequently to the cables where they are apt to bind on the lever mechanism; tilt the handlebars so that oil runs into the cable casings. Oil all control levers and cable nipples. When fitting new cables and casings, charge the latter with grease. To inject grease, use a piece of rubber tube in conjunction with the grease-gun.

The Dipper Switch. It is permissible about every 5,000 miles to apply a little *thin oil* to the moving parts of the dipper switch, but apply only a *few* drops or you may cause a short-circuit in the lighting system.

CORRECT LUBRICATION

The Foot Gear-change. Apply the grease-gun about every 500 miles to the nipple shown at (7) in Fig. 4. On the 1965 and later "Continental G.T." model the gear-change lever pedal should be greased about every 500 miles. Also do not forget to grease the gear-change lever shaft. A nipple is provided for each item.

Brakes. About every 500 miles inject grease through the nipple provided for lubricating the rear-brake pedal. Oil the exposed front-brake cable and the rear-brake-rod joints at the same time.

The Rear Suspension. The Girling oil-damped units are leakproof and do not attempt to dismantle, drain, or replenish the suspension units with damping oil. Where nipples are provided, every 500 miles apply the grease-gun to lubricate the swinging-arm pivot.

After a very big mileage some annoying squeaking may come from the Girling rear-suspension units. This indicates that their spring shields require internal cleaning and greasing. Except in the case of the 1965-6 "Continental G.T." model, which has no dirt shields fitted, deal with each Girling unit in the following manner.

Cleaning and Greasing Girling Dirt Shields. To do this it is necessary to remove each rear-suspension unit from the frame. First see that the three-phase cam adjustment is set to give minimum loading on the internal spring as shown at *A* in Fig. 63. Secure the lower end of the suspension unit in a vice and grasp the top dirt-shield with both hands so as to compress the internal spring. This enables the split collar on top of the upper shield to be removed. Then slowly reduce the pressure exerted on the upper shield and remove it, and also the spring and lower shield. Clean and smear the insides of both dirt shields with suitable grease (*see* page 36) and reassemble the Girling suspension-unit.

When assembling the Girling unit, compress its spring as when dismantling it and replace the split collar on top of the dirt shield. Make sure that the two halves of the collar are correctly located with their outer edges contacting the top shield and with their inner edges under the upper cap. Finally replace the Girling unit in the frame of the motor-cycle. Note that a Girling rear-suspension unit must *always* be kept in an *upright* position when not attached to the motor-cycle frame.

Centre Stand Pivot. Inject grease through the nipple provided about every 500 miles.

CHAPTER IV

LUCAS A.C. LIGHTING-IGNITION

THIS electrical system does not include a dynamo for charging the battery with d.c. current and the battery is not provided solely for lighting purposes as is the case where a dynamo and a separate magneto are included, the latter being used solely for ignition. The lighting and ignition systems are *combined* and the battery is used for lighting *and* ignition.

The System Briefly Explained. With the Lucas a.c. lighting-ignition system provided on all Royal Enfield motor-cycles dealt with in this handbook, the generator is an alternator which is fitted to the off-side flywheel mainshaft and during rotation it produces alternating (a.c.) current. This a.c. current is converted by a rectifier into uni-directional or direct (d.c.) current before charging the battery. The rectifier in effect functions like a non-return valve. From the battery in the tool-box d.c. current is conveyed direct to the lamps when the lighting-switch (*see* page 5) is switched on. With the engine running and the separate ignition switch (*see* page 4) switched on, d.c. current also flows from the battery to the contact-breaker and then through the ignition coil to the sparking plug. The ignition coil and contact-breaker are responsible for converting low-tension into high-tension current. A "fat" spark at the plug is necessary to fire the engine and the moment when the spark occurs is the moment when the contacts of the contact-breaker open.

The Lighting Switch and Battery Charging. When the lighting switch is turned to the "L" position with the engine running, two pairs of alternator coils are disconnected and only the third pair is in use; current is provided for trickle-charging the battery as well as for energizing the ignition coil. With the lighting switch in the "H" position the alternator output is increased by connecting all three pairs of coils in parallel, thereby providing current for the headlamp, tail and speedometer lights in addition to the ignition and a trickle-charge for the battery.

Emergency Starting. As mentioned on page 5, the ignition switch has an "EMG" (emergency) starting position for use if the battery is discharged or removed. With the ignition switch in the "EMG" position the alternator is connected directly to the ignition coil via the contact-breaker, the current thus by-passing the battery.

Note that if lighting is required with the battery disconnected, engine revolutions must be kept low to prevent an excessive rise in voltage. Note also that if the battery is removed an emergency start cannot be made unless the lead normally connected to the battery negative terminal is earthed. Remember too that an emergency start cannot be satisfactorily made unless the contact-breaker gap and ignition timing are correct. As soon as an emergency start is made turn the ignition switch to the normal running ("IGN") position.

THE ALTERNATOR AND RECTIFIER

The Lucas Alternator (Types RM13 and RM18). The alternator (*see* Fig. 18) comprises a rotor and a stator. The rotor is secured with a key and locking-nut to an extension of the off-side flywheel mainshaft, and the faces of its hexagon-steel core have six powerful permanent magnets

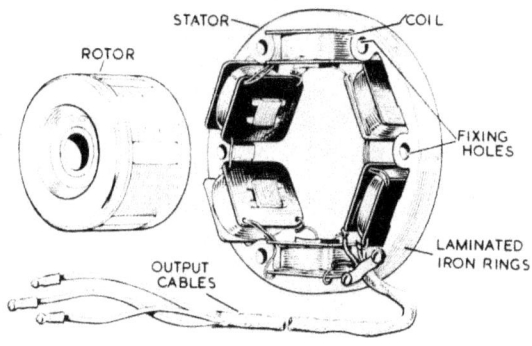

FIG. 18. THE ROTOR AND STATOR OF THE LUCAS RM13 ALTERNATOR
This alternator is fitted to all 1958–61 250 c.c. engines. The RM18 alternator fitted to all 1962–6 250 c.c. and all 350 c.c. engines is similar, but has a slightly greater output

arranged to produce six poles alternately north and south. Surrounding the rotor is the stator which is secured directly to the crankcase. The stator has three pairs of series-connected coils mounted on laminated iron-rings. An alternating current is produced in the stator coils by the rotation of the rotor in the centre of the stator and this a.c. current is passed on to the battery in the form of d.c. current via the rectifier.

The alternator itself requires no attention and rarely gives any trouble. When you have occasion to remove the off-side engine cover check that the three snap connectors in the output cables (*see* Fig. 18) are clean and tight, and that the cables are not frayed. In the unlikely event of alternator trouble occurring it is not advisable to meddle with the alternator yourself. Have the alternator inspected and attended to by a Lucas or Royal Enfield Service Agent.

If you do for any reason remove the rotor, note that it is not necessary to fit keepers to the rotor poles.

The Lucas Rectifier. Electrical connexion is made between the alternator-stator coils and a Lucas full-wave rectifier (*see* Fig. 19) clamped to a bracket below the tool-box as shown at (*11*) in Fig. 4. On the 1955 and later "Continental G.T." model the rectifier is enclosed (together with the ignition switch and coil) in a fibre-glass cover above the battery. The cover can be easily sprung off or on its three securing pins. The rectifier has four plates (coated with selenium) and, as previously mentioned, it converts a.c. current from the alternator to d.c. current for battery charging.

Keep the rectifier plates clean and its connexions tight. It is convenient

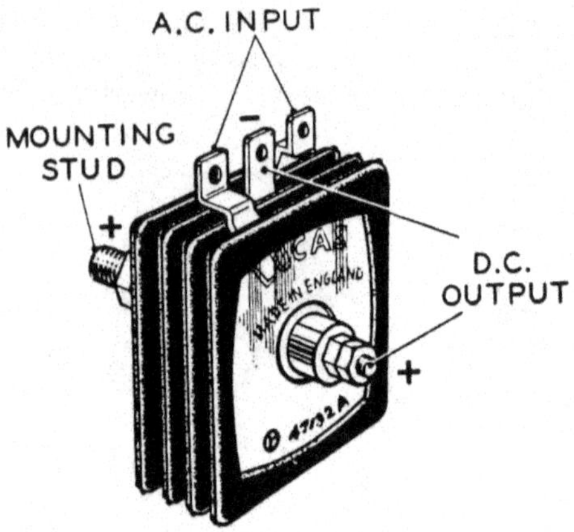

FIG. 19. THE LUCAS FULL-WAVE RECTIFIER
(*The Enfield Cycle Co. Ltd.*)

to use a small brush for removing any dust or dirt from the plates. Periodically check that the nut securing the rectifier to the bracket on the motorcycle is tight, but on no account slacken the nut which clamps the rectifier plates together to ensure correct rectifier performance. Be most careful not to connect the rectifier cables incorrectly. This can cause damage.

BATTERY MAINTENANCE

A Lucas-type PUZ7E or MLZ9E (1962 onwards) 6-volt battery is housed in the near-side of the tool-box. On the 1965–6 "Continental G.T." model, however, it is positioned below a quickly-detachable fibre-glass cover enclosing the ignition switch, the rectifier, and the coil. You can remove the battery without disturbing the cover. It is essential to keep the battery in really good condition by regular maintenance if it is to maintain its full capacity and enable the lamps to provide maximum trouble-free illumination at all times. The following points are extremely important—

1. Always keep the battery well charged.
2. Check the level of the electrolyte in the battery once a fortnight, and if necessary top-up the cells with distilled water to the correct level.
3. Keep the battery and its terminals clean, and the terminals tight.

4. See that the battery *earth* lead is always connected to the *positive terminal* of the battery.

5. If your Royal Enfield is to be out of service for a considerable period, fully charge the battery, remove it, and have it charged at a garage at fortnightly intervals.

New Batteries. These are supplied dry-charged and require filling with sulphuric acid of 1·270 or 1·260 density in the case of a PUZ7E or MLZ9E battery respectively. The former type battery may be identified by its black case, and the latter type by its white plastic case. Initial filling can conveniently be done by a Royal Enfield dealer or at a garage. A card giving appropriate initial filling instructions is attached to every new battery. After the initial filling the battery should be allowed to stand for one hour before being put into service.

Battery Charging. Note the remarks about the lighting switch and battery charging given on page 38. Where the battery is suspected to be under-charged, run as much as possible with the lighting switch in the "OFF" position so as to trickle-charge the battery without using any current except for ignition purposes.

Lead-acid batteries used with a.c. lighting-ignition sets lose their charge slightly more rapidly than dynamo lighting sets owing to a small leakage occurring through the rectifier. If you know that your motor-cycle will not be used for several days it is a good plan to disconnect the battery *earth* lead so as to prevent leakage through the rectifier. When leaving the machine standing with the engine stationary always be sure that the ignition is switched off, otherwise if the contacts of the contact-breaker happen to be closed some discharge may occur through the contact-breaker.

Topping-up the Battery Cells. About once a fortnight (more often in tropical climates) remove the battery from the near-side of the tool-box after disconnecting the battery strap (secured by one small screw), and the battery leads. On a PUZ7E type battery (*see* Fig. 20), clean the top of the battery and remove the three filler-plugs. Then examine the level of the electrolyte in each cell. When doing this do not hold a naked light near the filler-plug holes. If the level is below the top edges of the separators add distilled water as required with a Lucas battery filler (*see* Fig. 21) to bring the level correct. This should be done just *before* a charge run, as the agitation due to running and the gassing will thoroughly mix the solution. Insert the nozzle of the battery filler into each cell until the nozzle rests on the separators. Hold the filler in this position until the air bubbles stop rising in the glass container. The cell is then topped up to the correct level.

The PUZ7E type battery has, as may be seen in Fig. 20, an acid-level device and instead of using a Lucas battery filler you can, if you wish, use this device when topping-up each battery cell. Pour distilled water round its flange (not down the tube) until no more drains through into the cell. This occurs when the level of the electrolyte reaches the bottom of the central tube and prevents further escape of air displaced by the topping-up

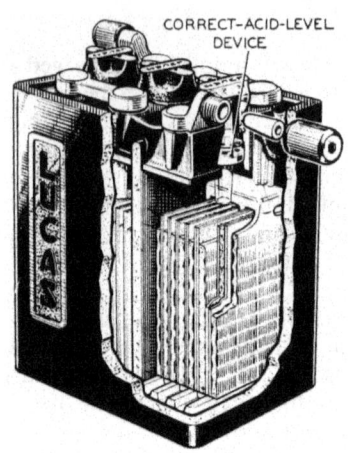

FIG. 20. CUT-AWAY VIEW OF THE LUCAS-TYPE PUZ7E BATTERY SHOWING INTERNAL DETAILS
(*The Enfield Cycle Co. Ltd.*)

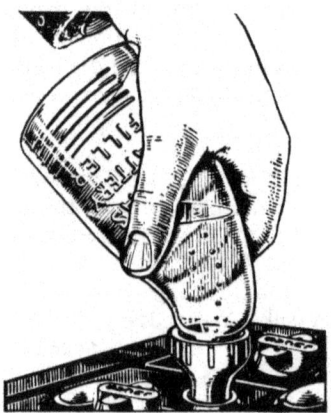

FIG. 21. TOPPING-UP A CELL WITH THE LUCAS BATTERY FILLER
(*The Enfield Cycle Co. Ltd.*)

water. Lift the tube slightly to permit the small quantity of water in the flange to drain into the cell; the level of the electrolyte will then be correct. Do not add acid to the electrolyte unless some of the sulphuric acid solution has been accidentally spilled.

Where an MLZ9E type battery (*see* Fig. 22) is provided it is not necessary to remove the filler-plugs in order to check the level of the electrolyte. The level can be observed through the semi-transparent plastic case. Top-up with distilled water (obtainable from most garages and chemists) if the electrolyte level is below the coloured line (*see* Fig. 22) marked "MAXIMUM ACID LEVEL" on the side of the battery case. If topping-up is

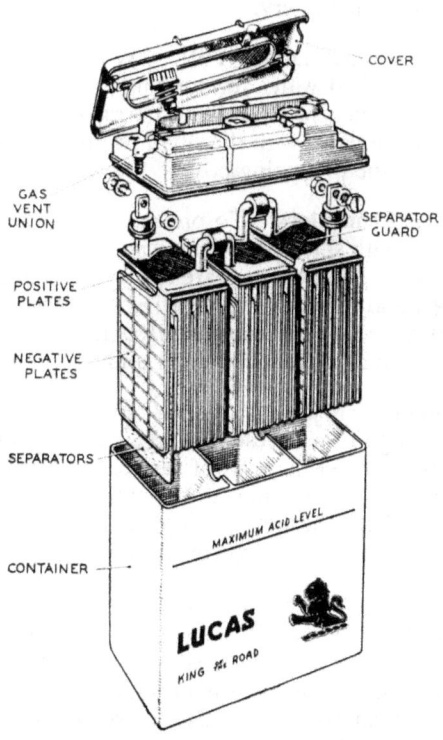

FIG. 22. EXPLODED VIEW OF LUCAS-TYPE MLZ9E BATTERY
(*The Enfield Cycle Co. Ltd.*)

necessary, do it as follows, and before a run to ensure proper mixing of the solution.

Remove the three filler-plugs from the top of the battery after removing the battery cover. Then with a suitable syringe insert distilled water through each filler-plug hole until the electrolyte level is up to the coloured line previously mentioned. Never top-up above this line, and note that a Lucas battery filler is quite unsuitable for topping-up an MLZ9E type battery.

After Topping-up the Battery. Before replacing each filler plug make sure that its vent hole is clear. A choked vent will result in an increase in pressure in the cell owing to "gassing" and this can cause trouble. Remove any dirt with a bent wire and also wipe the top of the battery thoroughly clean. Check that the rubber sealing washer for each filler plug is in sound condition and tighten down all three filler plugs securely. Finally replace the cover on an MLZ9E type battery (*see* Fig. 22), reposition and secure the battery.

Replenishing the Lucas Battery Filler. When replenishing a Lucas battery filler with distilled water for topping-up a type PUZ7E battery, see that the screw-on nozzle is replaced correctly. The rubber washer must be fitted over the valve with the small peg in the centre of the valve engaging the hole in the projecting boss of the washer.

Battery Terminal Connexions. To prevent corrosion it is a good plan to coat them lightly with some petroleum jelly. Always keep the connexions clean and tight. The terminals are clearly marked to indicate which is the positive (+) and which is the negative (−) terminal. The *positive* terminal must always have its cable *earthed* to the motor-cycle frame. Wrong connexion can damage the rectifier and alternator.

Storage Precautions. If you lay up your motor-cycle for a considerable period, see that it is given a refresher charge from a garage charger every two to three weeks. When left out of service, lead-acid batteries slowly discharge, and batteries left standing for long periods without being charged deteriorate, their plates becoming sulphated and often permanently spoiled. Never remove the electrolyte from a battery placed in storage.

THE LAMPS

All 250 c.c. and 350 c.c. models except the "Crusader Super 5," the "Olympic," and the "Continentals" have Lucas-type MCF 700 light-units, with a "pre-focus," double-filament main bulb, built into the "casquette" fork head which, as shown in Fig. 24, houses twin parking lights, the ammeter, the lighting switch, and also the speedometer.

On the "Crusader Super 5" and the "Olympic" a Lucas-type MCF 700P light-unit with a "pre-focus" double-filament main bulb, and a single parking bulb, is built into the "casquette" fork head.

The "Continental" models have a separate headlamp mounted on the front forks by a bracket and this headlamp has a Lucas-type MCF 700P light-unit with a "pre-focus" double-filament main bulb and a single parking bulb.

Lighting Switch Positions. *See* page 5.

The Lucas Light-unit (All models). The MCF 700 and the MCF 700P light-units are identical except that the MCF 700P type has a parking bulb which is a push fit in the rear of the reflector (see Fig. 23). The lens and reflector are sealed together and cannot be separated. This arrangement ensures that the lens and reflector are permanently protected and that the light-unit maintains its high efficiency for a long period. The light-unit can, however, be detached from the front rim if necessary. Fitted to the bulb holder at the rear of the reflector and secured by an adapter is the double-filament "pre-focus" main bulb. This bulb can be fitted in one position only and its filaments are accurately positioned in

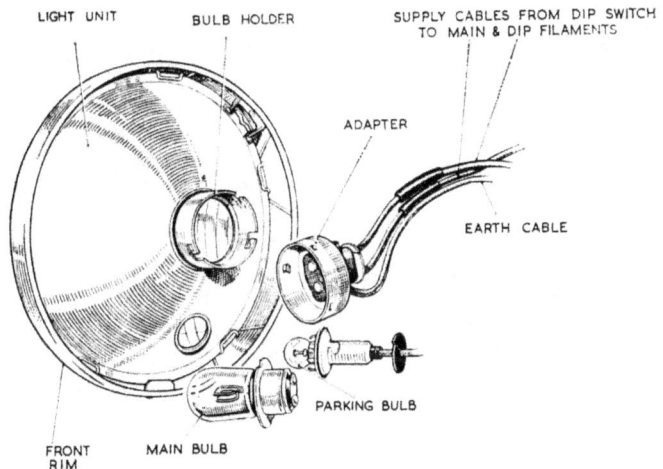

FIG. 23. THE LIGHT-UNIT REMOVED FROM A "CASQUETTE" FORK HEAD OR HEADLAMP ("CONTINENTAL" MODEL)

The main and parking bulbs are also shown withdrawn from the light-unit. The parking bulb shown is replaced by twin parking lights (see Fig. 24) on many Royal Enfields

relation to the reflector. This ensures that the light from the bulb is correctly focused, and no focusing adjustment is therefore necessary or provided.

"**Pre-focus**" **Main Bulb Renewal (All models).** First remove the light-unit assembly and front rim from the "casquette" fork head, or from the separate headlamp provided on the "Continental" models. To do this, loosen the screw at the top of the rim and carefully withdraw the rim and the attached light-unit assembly. The wiring for the double-filament main bulb, and also for the parking bulb (some models) will, of course, remain attached to the adapter (see Fig. 23). To remove the double-filament "pre-focus" main bulb, push the adapter inwards, turn it *anti-clockwise*, pull the bayonet-fixing adapter off, and remove the bulb from its holder in the rear of the reflector.

Fit a new "pre-focus" double-filament 6-volt, 30/24 watt Lucas No. 312

main bulb into the bulb holder. It can be fitted in one position only as a notch on its broad locating flange engages a projection in the bulb holder. Then engage the projections on the inside of the adapter with the slots in the bulb holder and secure the adapter by turning it *clockwise* while pressing it inwards. Having renewed the main bulb, replace the front rim with the attached light-unit assembly in the "casquette" fork head or (on the "Continental" models) the headlamp shell and securely tighten the rim fixing-screw.

Parking Bulb Renewal. Where the parking bulb has a holder pressed into the rear of the light-unit reflector (as on the "Crusader Super 5" and

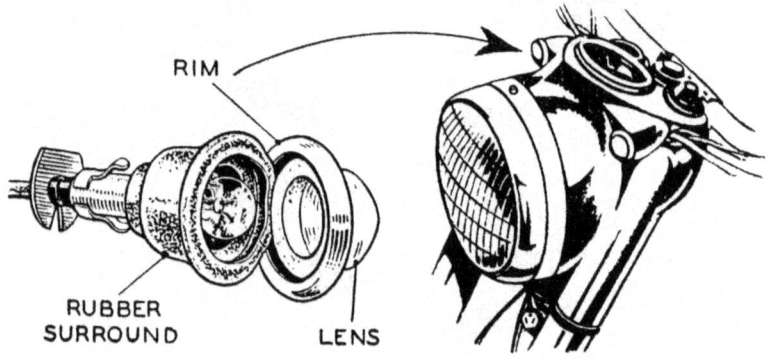

FIG. 24. SHOWING DETAILS OF ONE OF THE TWIN PARKING LIGHTS HOUSED IN THE "CASQUETTE" FORK HEAD

Fitted to all 1958-66 models except the "Crusader Super 5," the "Olympic," and the "Continental" models which have a single parking bulb as shown in Fig. 23
(*The Enfield Cycle Co. Ltd.*)

"Continental" models), remove the light-unit from the "casquette" fork head or the headlamp shell, as the case may be, using the procedure previously described. Pull the sprung holder out, complete with its bulb. When withdrawing the holder be careful not to lose the rubber washer.

On models with twin parking lights built into the "casquette" fork head (i.e. on all except the "Crusader Super 5," "Olympic," and "Continental" models) access to each parking bulb is obtained by removing the parking light rim (*see* Fig. 24). Pull the rim and lens from the rubber surround after removing the small security-screw. Then remove the faulty bulb and push a new Lucas 6-volt 3-watt M.B.C. parking bulb into the surround. Finally replace the lens and force the rim over the edge of the rubber surround. Do not forget to replace and tighten the small security-screw.

The Stop-tail Lamp (Type 564). This lamp (*see* Fig. 25) is provided on most Royal Enfields and has a reflex red reflector and a double-filament bulb. One 3-watt filament is used for the normal rear light and number plate illumination, and another 18-watt filament for the stop light to indicate when the motor-cycle is braking. The bulb holder has staggered slots to ensure correct fitting of the bulb. Note that it is most important to *see that the stop-tail lamp leads are correctly connected*, otherwise trouble as regards lamp illumination and battery discharge will occur.

Stop-tail Lamp Bulb Renewal. To obtain access to the double-filament bulb, remove the two captive screws (*see* Fig. 25) and withdraw the red moulded plastic cover. Then remove the double-filament bulb from its

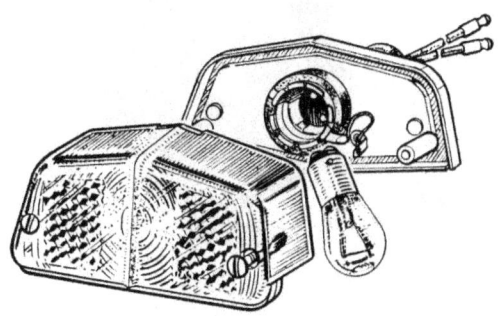

FIG. 25. THE LUCAS TYPE 564 STOP-TAIL LAMP WITH PLASTIC COVER AND BULB REMOVED

holder. On 250 c.c. machines fit a new 6-volt 3/18 watt Lucas No. 352 bulb. On 350 c.c. models the correct renewal bulb is a 6-volt 6/18 watt Lucas No. 384 bulb. Afterwards replace the red moulded plastic cover and secure it to the lamp body with the two captive screws.

The Speedometer Light. The bulb holder is accessible when the knurled ring is removed. Where a new bulb is required, fit a 6-volt, 1·8-watt (0·3 amp) bulb.

THE LUCAS ELECTRIC HORN

Horn Trouble. Note that uncertain horn action, resulting in a choking sound or complete failure of the diaphragm to vibrate, does not necessarily mean that there is a defect in the horn itself. Possibly a short-circuit has occurred in the electrical cable to the horn, a connexion is loose, the horn-push bracket makes poor electrical contact with the handlebars, or the battery is discharged. Slackness of the horn attachment to the frame can also upset the performance of the horn. If you find that none of the above possible causes of horn trouble exist, make an adjustment as described below. If trouble still persists return the horn to a Lucas Service Depot for examination.

To Adjust Type HF1849. This type of horn is fitted to 1958–61 250 c.c. models and a small adjustment may be necessary at infrequent intervals to ensure that the horn continues to function satisfactorily.

To make an adjustment, referring to Fig. 26, first remove the cover (held by a single screw) and the retaining strap from the back of the horn.

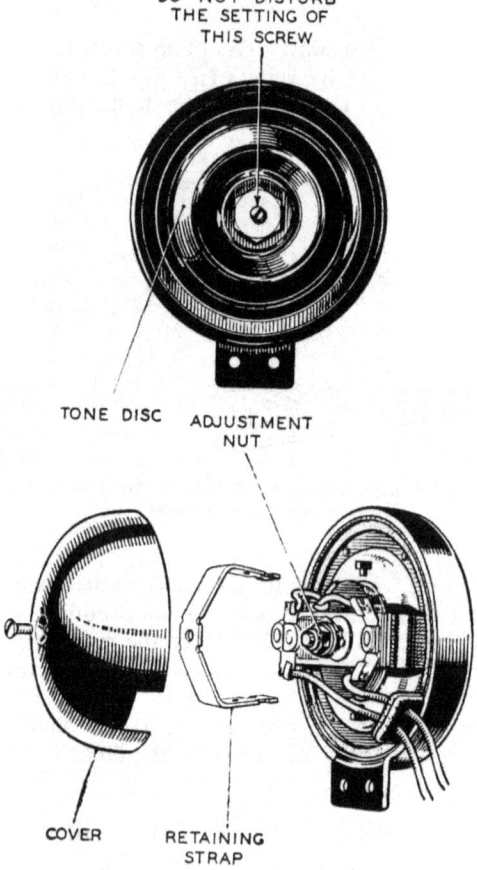

FIG. 26. THE LUCAS TYPE HF1849 ELECTRIC HORN WITH ITS REAR COVER REMOVED FOR CONTACT-BREAKER ADJUSTMENT

Inspect the contact-breaker contacts and, if they are burned or blackened, clean them with a fine file or emery cloth. Then operate the horn and with a 2BA spanner turn the adjusting nut *clockwise* until the horn just fails to sound. Afterwards turn the adjusting nut *anti-clockwise* until the best horn performance is obtained. As indicated in Fig. 26, do not disturb the slotted screw in the centre of the tone disc.

LUCAS A.C. LIGHTING-IGNITION   49

To Adjust Type 8H. This type of horn is fitted to 1962-6 250 c.c. models and to the 1963-5 "350 Bullet." As with the type HF1849 horn, an adjustment may be required very occasionally. To take up wear of the moving parts of the horn a small serrated adjustment-screw is located at the back of the horn near the terminal blades. To obtain the best horn performance, turn the screw *anti-clockwise* until the horn just fails to respond, and then turn it back one-quarter to half a turn.

THE IGNITION SYSTEM

As has been mentioned on page 38, a.c. current from the Lucas alternator charges the battery via the rectifier which converts the a.c. current to d.c. current. With the engine rotating, some current from the battery passes through the contact-breaker and the ignition coil to the sparking plug. The contact-breaker and the coil convert low-tension current into high-tension current to give a "fat" spark at the sparking plug. The opening of the contact-breaker contacts sees to it that the spark occurs at the right time, that is when the piston almost reaches top-dead-centre on its compression stroke.

The Ignition Switch. The use of this switch is dealt with on page 4.

Emergency Starting. Starting the engine with the ignition switch in the "EMG" position when the battery is discharged or removed is referred to on page 5.

Suitable Sparking Plugs. To obtain easy starting and maximum engine performance throughout the throttle range it is always essential to run with a suitable sparking plug fitted. The Enfield Cycle Co. Ltd. recommend the following types—
Lodge—Fit a 14 mm. non-detachable type 2HN or 3HN (a type 3HN only on the "Crusader Sports," "Continental," "Continental G.T.," and "Crusader Super 5").
K.L.G.—Fit a 14 mm. detachable type F80 (a detachable type F100 on the "Crusader Sports," "Continental," "Continental G.T.," "Olympic," and "Crusader Super 5").
Champion—Fit a 14 mm. non-detachable type L7 (a non-detachable type L5 on the "Crusader Sports," "Continental G.T.," "Continental," and "Crusader Super 5").
The above-mentioned types of sparking plugs are recommended after careful road and bench tests have been made, and the recommended types should remain serviceable for a long time, provided that regular attention is given to cleaning and checking the gap between the plug points. Note that the non-detachable type Lodge and Champion plugs cannot be dismantled for cleaning. To prevent water getting on a plug terminal and causing a short, always see that a waterproof terminal cover is provided.

MAINTENANCE OF IGNITION SYSTEM

The Lucas RM13 or RM18 Alternator. No maintenance is necessary (*see* page 39).

The Lucas Rectifier. Observe the brief instructions given on page 40.

The Lucas Type PUZ7E or MLZ9E Battery. Battery maintenance must be regularly attended to and comprehensive instructions are given on pages 40–4.

The Ignition Coil. The Lucas type MA6 coil is clipped inside the rear of the tool-box (*see* Fig. 4) and requires no maintenance other than to check occasionally that the terminal connexions are tight and that the electrical leads are in good condition. On the 1965 and later "Continental G.T." model the ignition coil is housed (together with the ignition switch and rectifier) in a fibre-glass cover above the battery. It is a simple matter to spring off the cover from the three pins securing it.

Keep the Sparking-plug Gap Correct. This is important because the points of the electrodes gradually burn away, thus enlarging the gap and causing a tendency for difficult starting and poor slow-running. Check the gap between the centre electrode and the outer earthed point regularly about every 2,000 miles, using a suitable feeler gauge obtainable from a motor-cycle dealer or accessory firm. The gauge should just pass between the points without springing them. On all 1958 and later single-cylinder O.H.V. Royal Enfield engines the correct sparking-plug gap is 0·018–0·025 in. For obvious reasons, when re-gapping a plug is necessary it is advisable to set the gap at or near the bottom limit.

If the sparking-plug gap is found to be excessive, press (not knock) the outer (earthed) point gently towards the centre electrode, using a plug re-gapping tool such as that shown in Fig. 27. Plug manufacturers supply this tool and it can be obtained from all accessory firms. A pair of snipe-nose pliers can be used for re-gapping, but it is preferable to use a proper re-gapping tool. Never attempt to bend or tap the centre electrode.

Keep the Sparking Plug Clean. A sparking plug is liable to become oiled up, sooty, or carbonized, or all three, and it is most important to keep the plug clean. If carburettor adjustment is correct and excessive oil is not entering the combustion chamber it should not be necessary to clean the sparking plug thoroughly more often than every 3,000 miles. When running-in a new or rebored engine it is advisable, however, to remove and check the plug for cleanliness after covering 500 miles.

Quick cleaning of a sparking plug in reasonably good condition can be effected by brushing the plug points with a small wire brush and lightly rubbing their firing sides with some smooth emery-cloth. Alternatively a plug can be cleaned with a proprietary gadget. Thorough cleaning of a sparking plug which has become very dirty is always desirable, and as previously stated should be done every 3,000 miles.

Thorough Cleaning (Non-detachable-type Plugs). Non-detachable type sparking plugs such as the Lodge 2HN or 3HN and the Champion L5 or L7 cannot be dismantled for thorough cleaning. A non-detachable sparking plug should be removed and handed to a garage for cleaning and testing with the special equipment provided at service garages. With this equipment the plug can in a few minutes be thoroughly cleaned of all

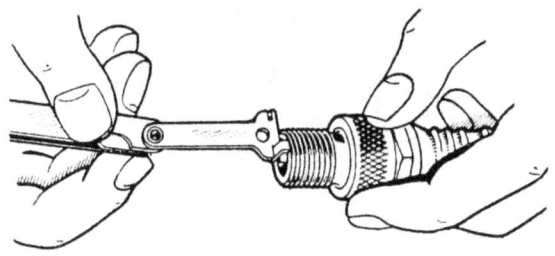

FIG. 27. USING A TYPICAL SPARKING PLUG RE-GAPPING TOOL
This type of tool includes feeler gauges for checking the sparking-plug gap

deposits, washed, and tested for sparking at a pressure exceeding 100 lb per sq in. *All* sparking plugs can now be cleaned quickly in this manner.

Thorough Cleaning (Detachable-type Plugs). A detachable-type sparking plug such as the K.L.G. F80 or K.L.G. F100 can readily be dismantled for thorough cleaning. Dismantling and cleaning should be done in the following manner if you do not avail yourself of garage equipment—

Referring to Fig. 28, hold the smaller hexagon of the gland nut *B* in a vice or with a suitable spanner. If you use a vice, be most careful not to exert any pressure on the hexagon faces. Then with a suitable box-spanner applied to the larger hexagon *E* of the plug body, unscrew the body until it is separated from the gland nut. The centre electrode *F* with its insulation (comprising the insulated electrode assembly *A*) can now be detached from the gland nut. Be careful not to lose the internal sealing washer *H*.

To clean the insulation, wipe it clean with a cloth soaked in petrol or paraffin. If the insulation is coated with hard-carbon deposits, remove these with some fine emery-cloth, but make no attempt to scrape off the deposits. The internal sealing washer *H*, and the surfaces of the insulator and in the metal body on which the washer rests, are very important as they prevent gas leakage through the sparking plug. Therefore wipe them only with a cloth soaked in petrol or paraffin.

To clean the metal parts (the plug body and gland nut), wipe them clean with petrol, or if necessary, scrape off carbon deposits with a small knife,

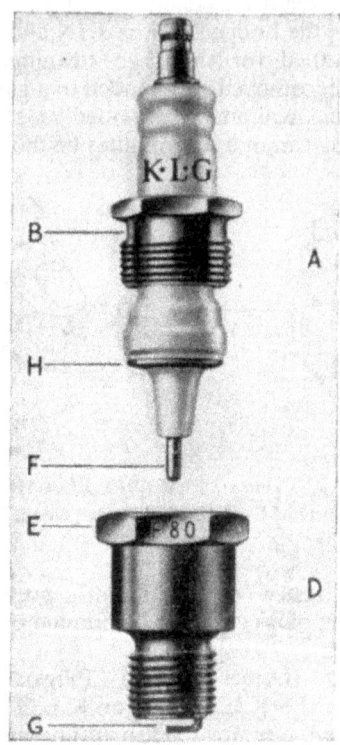

FIG. 28. A DETACHABLE-TYPE SPARKING PLUG DISMANTLED FOR THOROUGH CLEANING

The insulated electrode assembly *A* is shown with the internal sealing washer *H* and the gland nut *B* in position

or use a wire brush. Afterwards rinse the parts in petrol. The gland nut seldom gets very dirty and the same may apply to the external threads of the sparking plug. Clean and polish the points of the centre and outside (earth) electrodes *F* and *G* with some fine emery-cloth.

Check that there is no grit or dirt lodged between the body of the sparking plug and the insulation, and especially on the internal sealing washer and contacting faces. Smear a little thin oil on the internal sealing washer and make certain that it seats properly.

When reassembling the sparking plug, make sure that the centre electrode and insulation are positioned centrally in the body of the core. If they are not, remove, re-position while rotating the insulation a quarter of a turn, and reassemble. Do not attempt to force it into position or bend it.

Replacing the Sparking Plug. Prior to screwing the plug home into the cylinder head, renew its copper washer if this is flattened or worn, and clean the plug threads with a wire brush. It is a good plan to coat the threads with some graphite paste as this facilitates subsequent removal. Screw the plug home by hand as far as possible, and always use the box-spanner in the tool kit for final tightening. Do not employ excessive force, and never use an adjustable spanner for final tightening, as this can cause distortion.

Simple Method of Testing Plug and H.T. Lead. Switch on the ignition. Then to test that high-tension current reaches the plug end of the H.T. lead, rotate the engine quickly with the kick-starter while applying a wooden-handled screwdriver blade to the plug terminal and close to the cylinder head. Observe if sparks occur regularly. To test the sparking plug, lay it on the cylinder head with the H.T. lead connected, and the plug metal body in contact with the head, and observe whether the plug sparks properly while rotating the engine. The above procedure is recommended where an engine obstinately refuses to start.

Check Contact-breaker Gap Every 6,000 Miles. Check the gap between the contacts of the Lucas-type CA1A contact-breaker after covering 500 miles on a new machine, and subsequently every 6,000 miles. It is very important to maintain the correct gap which is 0·014–0·016 in. An incorrect gap affects the ignition timing and spoils engine performance.

To check the contact-breaker gap, first remove the small circular cover from the crankcase off-side cover (*see* Fig. 4). It has two securing screws. Also rotate the engine slowly forward with the kick-starter, or by means of the rear wheel with a gear engaged, until the contacts (*see* Fig. 29) are wide open (i.e. with the piston near T.D.C. on the compression stroke). Then, with the ignition switched off, insert an appropriate feeler gauge between the contacts. It should slide in without friction if the gap is correct.

If the contact-breaker gap is found to be too small or too large, make the necessary adjustment in the following manner. Referring to Fig. 29, with the contacts (*B*) still wide open, first slightly loosen the two screws (*C*) which secure the contact carrier-plate (*F*) to the contact-breaker base plate (*E*). Then adjust the position of the contact carrier-plate, which swivels around the pivot of the rocker arm (*G*), until the correct contact-breaker gap is obtained. Afterwards firmly tighten the two screws (*C*) and again check the gap between the contacts. Finally replace the small circular cover on the crankcase cover.

Cleaning the Contacts of the Contact-breaker. When checking the contact-breaker gap every 6,000 miles, also carefully examine the condition of the contacts. If their surfaces have a grey, frosted appearance with no blackening or pitting present, it is generally sufficient to clean the contacts with a cloth moistened with petrol. Make sure that there is no dirt, oil,

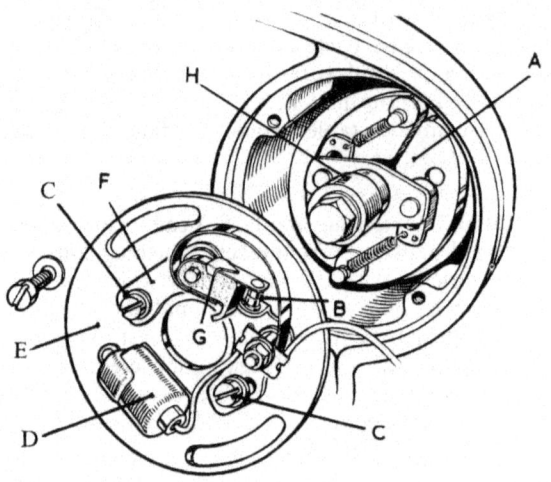

FIG. 29. THE CONTACT-BREAKER AND AUTOMATIC IGNITION-ADVANCE MECHANISM

The contact-breaker base plate is shown removed from the housing for the automatic ignition-advance mechanism. Note that the cam which operates the contact-breaker is on the same shaft as the oil pump located on the opposite side of the crankcase. The shaft (*see* Fig. 42) is gear-driven from the camshaft at half engine speed

- *A.* Automatic ignition-advance mechanism
- *B.* Contacts
- *C.* Screws securing contact carrier-plate *F* to base plate *E*
- *D.* Condenser
- *E.* Contact-breaker base plate
- *F.* Contact carrier-plate
- *G.* Rocker arm
- *H.* Cam operating *G*

(*The Enfield Cycle Co. Ltd.*)

or grease on or near the contacts. Dirty contacts rapidly become burnt and pitted.

If the contact surfaces are found to be *very* slightly blackened or pitted it is generally possible to clean both contacts with some *fine* emery-cloth inserted between the contacts, but where appreciable blackened areas and pitting are observed the rocker arm (*see* Fig. 29) carrying the moving contact should be removed, complete with spring. Then clean and polish both contacts most carefully, using a *fine* carborundum slip or a piece of *fine* emery-cloth. Continue cleaning the contacts until all blackening and pitting disappears and the contact surfaces are smooth all over. Be careful to keep the contact faces "square," and avoid removing excessive metal.

If a reasonable amount of facing-up fails to restore the contact faces to normal, fit a new pair of contacts (including, of course, a new rocker arm). After cleaning is completed, replace the rocker arm carrying the moving contact. Before doing this smear its pivot lightly with some grease and when replacing the rocker-arm spring make sure that it is below the fibre washer, i.e. between the fibre washer and the wiring tag from the condenser. Finally check the contact-breaker gap as previously described, and replace the contact-breaker cover on the crankcase.

IGNITION TIMING (ALL MODELS)

Symptoms of Incorrect Ignition Timing. Symptoms of an excessively *advanced* ignition timing are: (a) difficult starting with a tendency for the engine to back-fire and give the kick-starter a nasty jolt in the wrong direction; (b) poor slow-running; (c) a tendency for pre-ignition or "pinking" when running at moderate speeds. When travelling fast, the engine may run quite well, though a little harshly. Running with the ignition excessively advanced, especially at low and moderate engine speeds, can have a most damaging effect on the big-end bearing because of combustion occurring *before* the piston reaches top-dead-centre (T.D.C.) on the compression stroke.

When considering whether "pre-ignition" or "pinking" is caused through running with the ignition timing excessively *advanced*, remember that this trouble can also be due to: (a) using an unsuitable petrol; (b) carburettor trouble; (c) carbon deposits on the piston crown; (d) a weak mixture due to air leaks; (e) running with an unsuitable sparking plug fitted; (f) an *excessive* contact-breaker gap.

Symptoms of an excessively *retarded* ignition timing are: (a) serious loss of power; (b) overheating, accompanied by a very hot exhaust-pipe in the vicinity of the exhaust port; (c) excessive petrol consumption; (d) a tendency for the engine to run well on small throttle openings, but badly on larger ones; (e) occasional banging in the exhaust pipe and silencer. Where symptoms of retarded ignition occur, consider the possibility of the valve clearances being *excessive*, or the contact-breaker gap *insufficient*. Valve clearance and contact-breaker adjustment are dealt with on pages 62 and 53 respectively, and should be regularly attended to.

Re-timing is Seldom Necessary. If symptoms of advanced or retarded ignition timing develop, do not jump to the conclusion that the ignition timing itself *is* at fault. Re-timing is seldom necessary unless the timing chain has become slack (*see* page 64), the timing has slipped, or the drives to the oil pump and the camshaft have been dismantled (*see* page 88). After a big mileage, however, wear of the contact-breaker contacts and the rocker arm affects the timing and the timing should be checked and if necessary adjusted. Check the ignition timing if the engine continues to run badly in spite of having been carefully and regularly attended to as regards routine maintenance.

The Correct Ignition Timing. The ignition timing is correct when the contacts of the contact-breaker commence to open with the piston $\frac{1}{64}$ in. before T.D.C. on the compression stroke with the *ignition fully retarded*. Because of the provision of automatic ignition-advance mechanism behind the contact-breaker (*see* Fig. 29) the ignition is always fully retarded when the engine is stationary or turning over slowly. Never use an ignition timing other than that just mentioned. This gives a *maximum* ignition advance of $\frac{7}{32}$ in. and $\frac{5}{16}$ in. before T.D.C. in the case of 250 c.c. and 350 c.c. engines respectively; $\frac{1}{64}$ in. equals 5° of crankshaft movement.

Before Checking the Ignition Timing. Check and if necessary adjust the contact-breaker gap (*see* page 53). See that the gap, with the contacts wide open, is set to 0·014–0·016 in.

Checking the Ignition Timing. As previously indicated, this is seldom necessary. To check the ignition timing, with the motor-cycle on its stand, adopt the following procedure. First switch off the ignition and remove the circular cover from the off-side crankcase cover. Also remove the rocker-box cover and the sparking plug. Then, with top gear engaged, rotate the engine slowly *forwards* by turning the rear wheel until the piston is at T.D.C. on the compression stroke (the upward stroke following the closing of the exhaust valve). Both valves should now, of course, be closed.

To find the exact T.D.C. position of the piston, insert a suitable length of stiff wire or rod, preferably the latter, through the sparking-plug hole until it rests on the piston crown with its upper end projecting several inches from the plug hole. Then rock the crankshaft to and fro until the piston is positioned so that slight rocking produces no movement of the wire or rod. The piston is now exactly at T.D.C. Scratch a mark on the wire or rod where it emerges from the sparking-plug hole to indicate the T.D.C. position.

Scratch another mark $\frac{1}{64}$ in. *above* the T.D.C. mark. Then rotate the engine slowly *backwards* until the top mark occupies the position of the bottom (T.D.C.) mark. The piston will then have obviously descended in the cylinder bore a distance of $\frac{1}{64}$ in. below T.D.C.

With the piston positioned $\frac{1}{64}$ in. before T.D.C. the contacts of the contact-breaker should commence to open, as indicated by a thin Cellophane slip or a piece of tissue paper inserted between the contacts being just released by a gentle pull. Alternatively switch on the ignition and note if the ammeter needle flicks over from zero to discharge immediately the piston is moved very slightly up or down. It should do so if the timing is correct. The first method is the safest.

Re-timing the Ignition. There are two methods of correcting the ignition timing. Where only a *slight* adjustment is necessary to compensate for worn contact-breaker contacts and/or a worn rocker arm, use procedure 1.

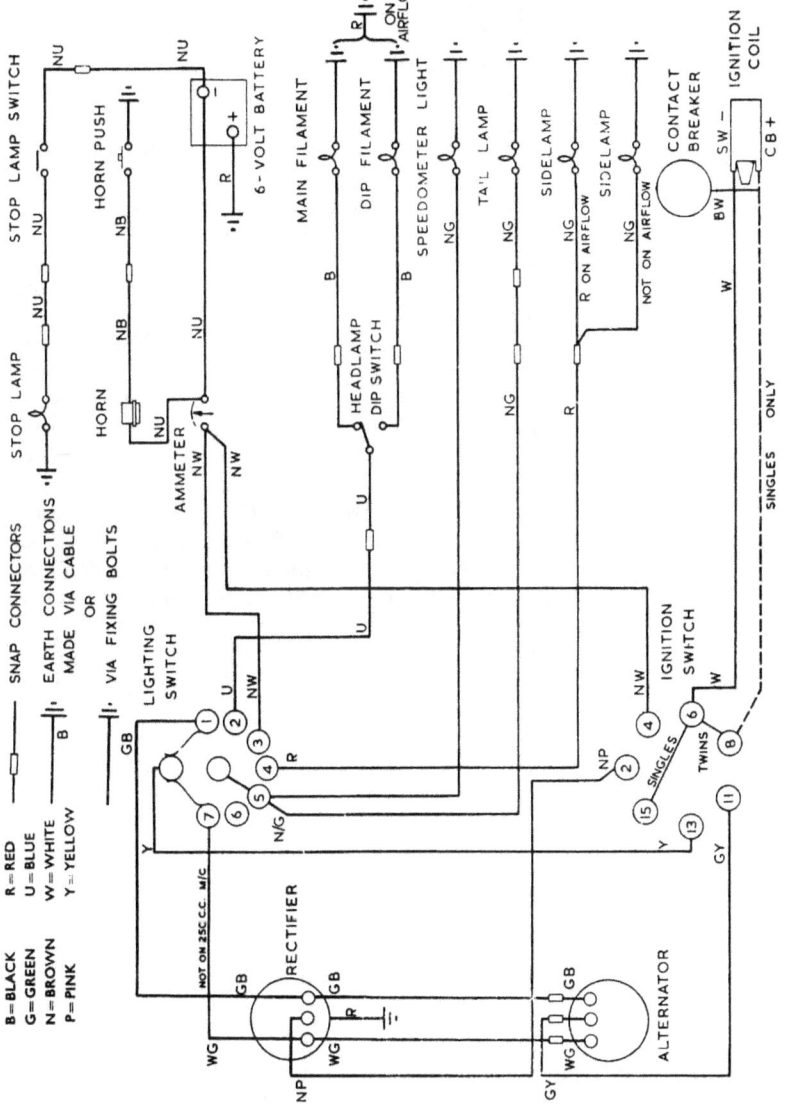

Fig. 30. Wiring Diagram for Lucas A.C. Lighting-Ignition System on 250, 350 C.C. Engines

Where a *considerable* adjustment is necessary *after the ignition timing has slipped or after a major overhaul*, use procedure 2.

Procedure 1. With the piston positioned $\frac{1}{64}$ in. (equivalent to 5 degrees on the crankshaft) before T.D.C., and referring to Fig. 29, loosen the two screws which secure the contact-breaker base plate (E) to the housing of the automatic ignition-advance mechanism (A), and turn the base plate clockwise (to advance) or anti-clockwise (to retard), as required, until the contacts (B) commence to open, using a Cellophane slip inserted between the contacts, or using the ammeter, to indicate the exact moment of "break." Then tighten the contact-breaker base plate securing-screws (C) and replace the rocker-box and contact-breaker covers.

Note that the above procedure provides a range of adjustment equal to $\pm$ 39 degrees on the crankshaft, sufficient for all likely wear of the contact-breaker contacts and rocker arm.

Procedure 2. Referring to Fig. 29, remove the screw which secures the contact-breaker cam (H) to its shaft and withdraw the cam. Slacken the screws (C) securing the contact-breaker base plate (E) to the housing of the automatic ignition-advance mechanism and set the base plate so that its two slots are centrally positioned relative to the base-plate securing-screws.

With the piston positioned at $\frac{1}{64}$ in. before T.D.C. on the compression stroke, turn the cam *clockwise* (viewed from the off-side of the motor-cycle) until the ammeter needle flicks over to zero, indicating that the contacts have begun to open. Alternatively use the method, previously described, of inserting a thin Cellophane slip or a piece of tissue paper between the contacts to indicate the exact moment when the "break" occurs. When the correct ignition timing is obtained, tighten the two contact-breaker base securing-screws and replace the rocker-box and contact-breaker covers.

CHAPTER V

GENERAL MAINTENANCE

THIS chapter contains *all* essential maintenance instructions for the 1958-66 250, 350 c.c. single-cylinder four-stroke O.H.V. Royal Enfields listed in the Preface of this handbook. Attend to routine maintenance regularly and carefully, and do not wait until your mount "screams" for attention! *In this chapter instructions not dated or not referred to as applying to particular models apply to all 1958-66 models.* Detailed references to carburation, lubrication, and the Lucas a.c. lighting-ignition system are not included, as these subjects have been previously dealt with in Chapters II, III, and IV respectively.

Spares and Repairs. Should you have occasion to forward or deliver any parts to the Service Dept. of The Enfield Cycle Co. Ltd. (phone: Redditch 121) or to an appointed spares stockist or repairer, attach to each part a label bearing clearly your full name and address. To facilitate the identification of a part or unit, always quote the year of manufacture and type of model (e.g. 1964 "Crusader Sports"), and also the engine or frame number (*see* page 2), according to which applies. Note that very useful illustrated spares lists are obtainable from the makers and from appointed spares stockists. The Enfield Cycle Co. Ltd. (Service Dept.) will be pleased to advise you as to the spares or repair specialist nearest to your address. The firm itself has, of course, an almost unlimited supply of spares and is always pleased to undertake any kind of repair work. Such repair work is done efficiently by those who really know their job.

The author would draw attention to a really excellent firm in London, namely E.S. Motors Ltd. of 319-325 High Road, Chiswick, W.4 (phone: Chiswick 2246). This firm stocks a vast quantity of Royal Enfield spares and has a quick C.O.D. service. It also sells new and second-hand Royal Enfields. Three other good London spares stockists are: Young's of 18-32 Tooting Bec Road, S.W.17 (phone: Balham 7791); Deeprose Bros. of 179, 184 Brownhill Road, S.E.6 (phone: Hit 8888); and O'Neil Bros. of 270 West Hendon Broadway, N.W.9 (phone: Hendon 8629). Good provincial spares stockists are: Reg Oakes of 95 Wakefield Road, Huddersfield; and John W. Groombridge of Cross-in-Hand, Heathfield, Sussex (phone: Heathfield 2466). Major overhaul of the power unit *and* motor-cycle are for obvious reasons best undertaken by the Service Dept. of The Enfield Cycle Co. Ltd.

Some Useful Accessory Firms. Among reputable large accessory firms (some of which have branches throughout the U.K.) handling motor-cycle accessories, proprietary tools, clothing, etc., may be mentioned: E.S. Motors Ltd.; Marble Arch Motor Supplies Ltd.; The Halford Cycle Co. Ltd.; Whitbys of Acton Ltd.; Pride & Clarke Ltd.; Turner's Stores; Kays of Ealing Ltd.; James Grose Ltd.; and George Grose Ltd.

Items Needed for Thorough Maintenance. For thorough maintenance you will need various items in addition to the standard tool-kit. These items include: a can of paraffin and a pail for cleaning purposes; a stiff brush for scouring dirt from under the engine-gearbox unit; a suitable receptacle for draining oil from the oil tank and engine sump; some non-fluffy rags for cleaning; some dishes and jars in which to wash components; a small funnel for topping-up the gearbox and front forks; an oil-can; a grease-gun such as the Tecalemit; a canister of suitable grease (*see* page 36); a tin of engine oil suitable for the engine and gearbox (*see* page 30); a chamois leather; some soft dusters; a sponge and pail (where no hose is available); and some good hand cleaner such as "Swarfega."

You should also obtain: a tyre pressure gauge (*see* page 101); a Lucas battery filler or syringe (*see* page 43) for topping-up the battery; a bottle containing distilled water; a set of engine gaskets; a tube of jointing compound such as red Hermatite; a good chromium-cleaning compound; a small wire brush for cleaning; some insulation tape; some good polish for the enamelled parts; some valve-grinding paste such as Richford's (coarse and fine); some fine emery-cloth, and a pair of new gudgeon-pin circlips.

In addition to the standard tool-kit you will need: a good set of feeler gauges for checking the valve clearances and sparking-plug and contact-breaker gaps; a rubber suction-type (or a metal type) valve holder for grinding-in the valves (*see* page 81); a valve spring compressor (*see* page 81); a gudgeon-pin extractor (*see* page 76); a pair of snipe-nose pliers for fitting circlips; a pair of medium-size cutting pliers; a good make of adjustable spanner; a small electrical screwdriver; a sparking-plug re-gapping tool (*see* page 51); and a fairly broad, blunt screwdriver or proprietary scraper for chipping off carbon deposits.

Many Special Tools are Available. For major overhaul work many special tools are available and can be obtained from Redditch or an appointed dealer. These tools include: a crankshaft assembly tool; a crankshaft extractor; a camshaft sprocket-extractor; a pump-disc lapping tool; valve-seat cutters; valve-guide mandrels; an inlet valve-seat arbor; and a clutch-centre extractor. Major overhaul work, however, is beyond the scope of this maintenance handbook and is not recommended for the average motor-cyclist who has neither the facilities, time, or equipment available to undertake this type of work.

When a major overhaul becomes necessary it is best to get the work done by an appointed Royal Enfield repair specialist or else to ride or send the machine to Redditch for attention. Royal Enfields, however, run for

GENERAL MAINTENANCE 61

very many thousands of miles before a major overhaul becomes necessary, *provided that general maintenance is properly attended to.*

CLEANING ENGINE AND MACHINE

Keep Your Mount Clean. Regular cleaning is very important as it protects and maintains the enamelled finish in good condition. If a motor-cycle remains dirty it becomes an eyesore, some rusting is likely, defects are apt to pass unnoticed, and there is rapid depreciation.

Cleaning the Engine-gearbox Unit. Scour all filth from its lower parts, using stiff brushes and paraffin, or one of the popular oil and grease solvents such as "Gunk." When dismantling, clean all parts with paraffin and lay them on a clean sheet of paper.

If the enamel on the cylinder-barrel fins and the cylinder-head fins (where of cast iron) becomes detached, paint the cast-iron fins with some proprietary cylinder black after cleaning them with a stiff brush dipped in paraffin. Rusted fins, besides looking shabby, appreciably reduce heat dispersion.

Cleaning Enamelled Parts. Do not attempt to remove mud from the enamelled surfaces when dry and caked, as this is liable to damage the enamel. Where a hose is available, direct a stream of water on the dirty surfaces, being careful not to allow water to get on vulnerable parts such as the electrical equipment and the carburettor. If a hose is not available, use a sponge and pail to soak the mud off. Disperse it with plenty of clean water. When a machine is extremely dirty, it is advisable to paint the enamelled surfaces over with a cleaning compound such as "Gunk" before cleaning them with water. A cloth moistened with turpentine can be used for removing tar spots.

After thoroughly washing all the enamelled surfaces, dry them with a chamois leather and afterwards polish them with some soft dusters and a good type of car polish, or a proprietary polish such as "Karpol."

"Dry weather" riders can keep a machine in almost showroom condition merely by rubbing over the enamelled surfaces with a paraffin-damped cloth, followed by a soft dry duster.

Cleaning Chromium-plated Surfaces. On no account use metal polish or paste, as this wears down the thin plating quickly. You can, however, use a good proprietary chromium-cleaning compound such as "Belco." The usual method of cleaning is to remove the tarnish (salt deposits) regularly with a damp chamois leather and then polish the chromium with a soft cloth.

To Reduce Tarnishing. It is a good plan during the winter to wipe over the chromium-plated surfaces occasionally with a soft cloth soaked in a proprietary anti-tarnish preparation such as "Tekall," obtainable from most accessory firms and garages in $\frac{1}{2}$ pt. and 1 pt. tins.

MISCELLANEOUS

Run-in a New Engine Very Carefully. A new or re-bored engine should be treated with the greatest care during the 500 mile running-in period. Avoid large throttle openings and high piston speeds, and make full use of the gearbox to avoid placing an excessive load on the engine. For more detailed advice on running-in, *see* page 11.

Check External Nuts and Bolts Regularly for Tightness. While running-in a new machine some "bedding down" of various parts usually occurs and it is occasionally advisable to check the tightness of the various external nuts and bolts. This applies particularly to the engine, wheels, petrol-pipe unions, and all oil plugs. Note that during the running-in period and after decarbonizing, the cylinder-head securing nuts are very likely to slacken off slightly.

Carburettor Adjustment and Maintenance. Chapter II contains full slow-running adjustment and general maintenance instructions for the Amal "monobloc" carburettor fitted to all 1958–66 250 and 350 c.c. engines. Slow-running adjustment is dealt with on page 19 and the correct carburettor settings are given on page 25. For advice on engine starting and emergency starting, see pages 7 and 5 respectively.

Lubrication. This all-important subject is dealt with in Chapter III. Engine lubrication and motor-cycle lubrication are dealt with on pages 26–34 and 34–7 respectively.

The Lucas a.c. Lighting-ignition System. Routine maintenance of the alternator, rectifier, battery, lamps, contact-breaker, ignition coil and sparking plug is fully dealt with in Chapter IV, which also contains instructions for re-timing the ignition (*see* pages 56-8).

VALVE CLEARANCES

The maintenance of correct clearances, *with the engine cold*, between the off-side overhead-rocker pads and the valve stems or valve stem end-caps (provided on earlier type engines) is extremely important. The lift of the valves, their proper seating, and to some extent precise valve timing, depend upon the valve clearances being correct.

Insufficient valve clearances must *always* be avoided as they are liable to cause damage to the valves (especially the exhaust valve), loss of compression, overheating, and a reduction in power output. Excessive valve clearances are likely to cause a decline in performance, accompanied by noise, and are also bad for the valves, though less likely to cause serious damage than insufficient clearances.

Check Valve Clearances Every 1,000 Miles. It is advisable to check the valve clearances on a new or reconditioned engine after covering 250 miles,

GENERAL MAINTENANCE 63

again at 500 miles, and subsequently every 1,000 miles. Always check the clearances after grinding-in the valves and immediately if loss of engine compression or excessive noise occurs.

To Check the Clearances. It is assumed that the engine is *cold*. Remove the rocker-box cover after unscrewing its single securing nut (*see* Fig. 35). Also remove the sparking plug to enable the engine to be rotated easily. Then, with top gear engaged, slowly turn the engine over forwards until the piston is at or near top-dead-centre (T.D.C.) on the compression stroke (the upward piston stroke following the closing of the exhaust valve). In this position the inlet and exhaust valves should *both* be fully closed.

If your engine has a cast-iron cylinder head, insert a 0·004 in. feeler gauge between the pad of the inlet rocker-arm and the inlet valve stem or valve stem end-cap, where fitted. It should just *slide in* without pressure if the valve clearance is correct. Similarly check the exhaust-valve clearance, using a 0·006 in. feeler gauge.

If your engine has an aluminium-alloy cylinder head, it is not necessary or practicable to check the inlet-valve clearance with a feeler gauge. The inlet push-rod should be just able to spin freely without any up-and-down movement being possible. To check the exhaust-valve clearance, insert a 0·002 in. feeler gauge between the exhaust rocker-arm pad and the exhaust-valve stem or valve stem end-cap where fitted. It should just enter without using any pressure.

To Adjust the Clearances. Where the inlet and/or exhaust-valve clearance is found to be insufficient or excessive, the following adjustment must be made. Referring to Fig. 31, with the piston at or near T.D.C. on the compression stroke, with both valves closed, and the engine *cold*, with a spanner hold the hexagon (the bottom one) on the top end of the push-rod, and with another spanner loosen the lock-nut immediately above it by turning the nut *anti-clockwise*. Then, still holding the push-rod steady with the spanner applied to its bottom hexagon, turn the push-rod cup *anti-clockwise* as required to reduce the valve clearance or *clockwise* to increase it. Afterwards tighten the lock-nut firmly against the push-rod hexagon while preventing the latter from turning. When turning the lock-nut clockwise for tightening (especially if the lock-nut is stiff on the threads of the push-rod cup), make sure that the push-rod cup does not also turn, or the adjustment will be spoiled.

After adjusting the inlet and/or exhaust-valve clearance as required, using the appropriate feeler gauge, or spinning the push-rod on an engine with an aluminium-alloy cylinder head to check the inlet-valve clearance, replace the sparking plug and the rocker-box cover. Examine the gasket for the cover and if damaged, renew it (*see* page 86).

THE TIMING AND PRIMARY CHAINS

As may be seen in Fig. 32, a sprocket secured to the camshaft (*2*) is driven by the duplex timing chain (*1*) from a smaller sprocket on the near-side flywheel mainshaft (*6*) at half engine speed. Behind the smaller sprocket on the same mainshaft is a second larger sprocket which drives the clutch sprocket with the primary chain (*3*). Both chains are automatically

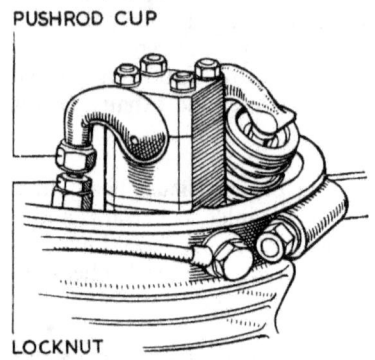

FIG. 31. THE PUSH-ROD ADJUSTMENT PROVIDED ON ALL ENGINES FOR OBTAINING CORRECT VALVE CLEARANCES

The rocker arm engaging the push-rod cup is on the near-side of the rocker-shaft bearing housing. On later type engines a single housing (*see* Fig. 36) replaces the two separate housings fitted to earlier type engines

(*The Enfield Cycle Co. Ltd.*)

lubricated with engine oil, and slipper-type chain tensioners (*4*), (*7*), with adjusters, are provided for maintaining the correct chain tension.

Checking and Adjusting Chain Tension. Every 2,000 miles when removing and cleaning the gauze filter, shown at (*9*) in Fig. 32, also check and if necessary adjust the tension of the duplex timing chain and the primary chain. Slackness of the timing chain slightly affects the ignition and valve timing, while slackness of the primary chain can cause undue wear of the sprocket teeth and some transmission snatch.

Referring to Fig. 32, to obtain access to the timing and the primary chains, remove the crankcase near-side cover (*see* page 32) after placing a tray beneath the engine to catch escaping oil. Then check the tension of the timing chain (*1*). With the chain correctly tensioned there should be a lateral movement of about $\frac{3}{16}$ in. on the front chain-run (i.e. on the side opposite to the slipper-type tensioner (*4*)). Should excessive slackness be present, loosen the two nuts (*5*) and move the slipper-type tensioner *anti-clockwise* until the correct chain tension is obtained. Afterwards firmly tighten the two nuts (*5*).

To check the tension of the primary chain (*3*) rotate the engine slowly

GENERAL MAINTENANCE 65

and while doing so check the tension of the top run of the chain by pressing the chain up-and-down with the fingers. The chain should not be tight

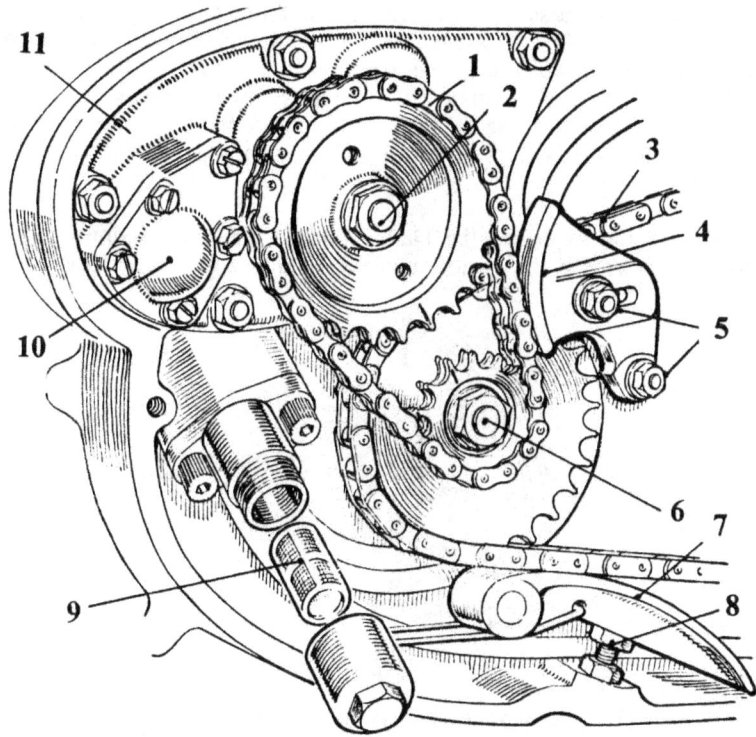

FIG. 32. SHOWING THE ADJUSTABLE SLIPPER-TYPE TENSIONERS FOR THE TIMING AND PRIMARY CHAINS, THE GAUZE OIL FILTER (WITHDRAWN), AND THE OIL PUMP ASSEMBLY

Access to all the components shown, as well as to the clutch, is obtained on removing the crankcase near-side cover (*see* Fig. 44). The duplex oil-pump shaft is gear-driven from the camshaft at half engine speed, and the contact-breaker cam on the opposite side of the crankcase is also attached to the same shaft, an unusual arrangement. Note the timing marks on the timing-chain sprockets

1. Timing chain (duplex)
2. Camshaft
3. Primary chain
4. Slipper-type tensioner for timing chain
5. Nuts for adjusting 4
6. Near-side flywheel mainshaft
7. Slipper-type tensioner for primary chain
8. Adjuster screw for 7
9. Oil-filter gauze element
10. Oil pump assembly
11. Cam-housing cover

(*The Enfield Cycle Co. Ltd.*)

and there should be about $\frac{1}{4}$ in. up-and-down movement with the chain in its tightest position. On most engines a screwed inspection cap is provided on the crankcase near-side cover and by removing this cap (shown at (*4*) in Fig. 54) it is possible to check the primary chain tension without removing the cover. But cover removal is, of course, necessary in order to make an adjustment of the slipper-type chain tensioner (*4*).

To take up slackness in the primary chain, referring to Fig. 32, unscrew the adjuster screw (*8*), as required, to raise the curved slipper-type tensioner (*7*) on which the lower run of the primary chain (*3*) rests, after loosening the lock-nut. When the chain has been correctly tensioned, tighten the lock-nut on the adjuster screw firmly and replace the crankcase near-side cover. Note the advice given on page 33 concerning the replacement of the cover.

Removing and Replacing the Timing Chain. The duplex timing chain, shown at (*1*) in Fig. 32, is not subjected to any appreciable load and is

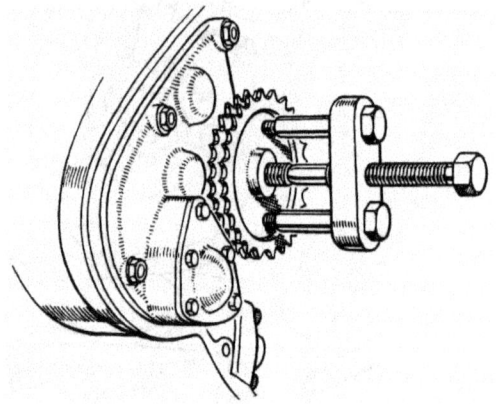

FIG. 33. WITHDRAWING CAMSHAFT SPROCKET WITH ROYAL ENFIELD EXTRACTOR
(*The Enfield Cycle Co. Ltd.*)

automatically lubricated. It therefore wears *very* slowly. Normally it becomes necessary to remove it only when the removal and renewal of the primary chain (*3*) is required after a big mileage. Remove the timing chain in the following manner.

First place a suitable tray beneath the engine to catch oil which will escape when the crankcase near-side cover is removed. Remove the cover as described in the paragraph on page 32 dealing with the removal of the gauze filter (*9*). Next remove the slipper-type tensioner (*4*) for the timing chain. With top gear engaged and the rear wheel prevented from turning by depressing the rear-brake pedal, remove the nut and washer from the end of the near-side flywheel mainshaft (*6*). Also remove the nut and washer from the end of the camshaft (*2*). Then withdraw the camshaft sprocket from the tapered end of the camshaft, using a camshaft sprocket extractor (Part No. E.4870) as shown in Fig. 33. The timing sprocket on the end

GENERAL MAINTENANCE

of the mainshaft has a parallel bore and can be readily withdrawn together with the camshaft sprocket and the timing chain. Be careful not to lose the small key provided on the camshaft to prevent the camshaft sprocket turning on its shaft (*see* Fig. 42).

When replacing the timing chain and sprockets it is essential to ensure the valve timing *and* ignition timing being correct, that the piston is at T.D.C. and that the small dash marks on the two sprockets are in line with each other and with the camshaft and mainshaft centres as shown in Fig. 32. Before replacing the camshaft sprocket make sure that the small key is in position. The slot in the end of the mainshaft is offset and therefore the timing sprocket cannot be put on the wrong way round. After replacing the two sprockets and the timing chain, replace the slipper-type tensioner and adjust the chain tension as described on page 64 until there is a lateral movement of about $\frac{3}{16}$ in. on the front chain-run. Afterwards replace the crankcase near-side cover (*see* page 33).

Removing and Replacing the Primary Chain. The primary chain, being completely enclosed and automatically lubricated, will run for many thousands of miles, provided its tension (*see* page 64) is maintained correct ($\frac{3}{4}$ in. up-and-down movement in the centre of the top chain run, with the chain in its tightest position). The chain is an endless type and it is therefore necessary to remove the chain together with the mainshaft and the clutch sprockets, using the following procedure—
1. Remove the crankcase near-side cover as described on page 32.
2. Remove the timing chain (*see* page 66) and its two sprockets.
3. Remove the slipper-type tensioner for the primary chain.
4. Dismantle the clutch (*see* page 92); withdraw the clutch sprocket after removing its large circlip and simultaneously remove the sprocket on the flywheel mainshaft together with the primary chain.

Fitting a new primary chain should be quite easy. Fit the chain together with the two sprockets and assemble the clutch plates. Replace the slipper-type primary-chain tensioner and then replace the timing chain and its two sprockets as previously described. See that the two sprocket timing marks are correctly positioned with the piston at T.D.C. Finally adjust both slipper-type tensioners to obtain correct chain tension (*see* page 64), and replace the crankcase near-side cover (*see* page 33).

THE DRY-SUMP SYSTEM

The Royal Enfield dry-sump system is most reliable and has no form of adjustment. Provided that the oil tank is topped-up regularly about every 200 miles with suitable engine oil, the tank and engine sump are both drained about every 2,000 miles, and the felt filter and gauze filter (where fitted) are cleaned at the same time, in accordance with the instructions given on pages 30–3, no trouble with the D.S. lubrication system is likely to occur.

Overhauling the Oil Pump. On rare occasions, usually after a very big mileage during which there is neglect as regards cleaning the filter(s) and draining the oil tank and engine sump, the oil pump fails to deliver oil properly due to wear of the pump disc and plungers. Failure to deliver oil can be checked by removing the oil filler cap with the engine running and observing whether oil returns properly through the oil-pressure relief valve.

To dismantle the oil pump where considered necessary for inspection, it is not necessary to remove the cam-housing cover. Remove the five

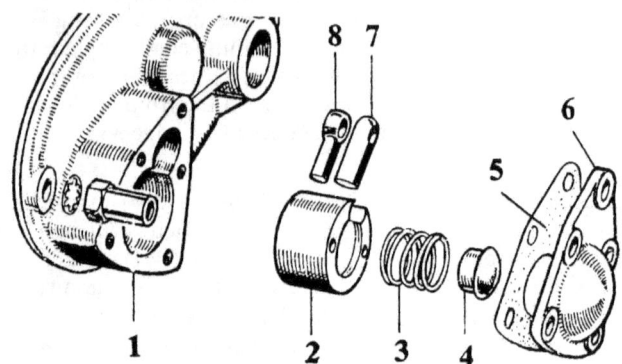

FIG. 34. SHOWING THE DUPLEX OIL PUMP REMOVED FROM ITS HOUSING IN THE CAM-HOUSING COVER

The oil-pump housing is integral with the cam-housing cover, and the latter is secured to the crankcase by five nuts

1. Oil-pump housing
2. Oil-pump disc
3. Disc spring
4. Spring end-cap
5. Oil-pump cover gasket
6. Oil-pump cover
7. Pump plunger (return)
8. Pump plunger (feed)

(*The Enfield Cycle Co. Ltd.*)

$\tfrac{3}{16}$ in. hexagon-headed screws (*see* Fig. 32) and withdraw the pump cover. Then remove the pump disc, the two plungers, the spring, and the spring cap from the pump housing (*see* Fig. 34).

Check the fit of the two plungers in the pump disc. It should be possible to move them in and out by hand, but the clearance should be *very small*. If when fitting a new disc or plungers, the latter are found to be too tight a fit, carefully lap them in with metal polish until they are just free. If the pump disc is not seating properly, or if a new disc is being fitted, lap the disc to its seating with the pump-disc lapping tool (Part No. E.6978), using Carborundum 360 fine paste or liquid metal-polish, until an even grey surface is obtained. Wash out thoroughly with petrol all passages in order to remove all traces of grinding paste, and then thoroughly oil the components.

GENERAL MAINTENANCE

Check the pump-disc spring for fatigue by assembling the pump in its housing and positioning the cover without tightening up. If the spring is serviceable the cover should be held not less than $\frac{1}{8}$ in. off its facing. The free length of the spring is $\frac{5}{8}$ in.

When assembling the oil pump, fit a new paper gasket if the old one is damaged, and do not use jointing compound. Tighten evenly and firmly the five pump-cover securing-screws, replace the crankcase near-side cover and afterwards check whether oil can be observed flowing through the oil-pressure relief valve when the tank filler-cap is removed. Note that a certain amount of air mixes with the oil because the capacity of the return pump is greater than the capacity of the feed pump.

The Crankcase Breather. On early models the breather is positioned on the front of the crankcase between the front engine plates, and it merely comprises a piece of synthetic rubber tube with a flattened end. If it does not operate efficiently it will cause smoking from the exhaust or over-oiling, and the obvious remedy is to fit a new breather. On later models the breather provided is *never* likely to require attention.

Oil-pressure Relief Valves. Early models have an oil-pressure relief valve in the oil feed to the big-end bearing (*see* Fig. 17). It comprises a body containing a $\frac{5}{16}$ in. steel ball and spring held in position by a plug. The plug should always be screwed home so that the face of the plug is level with the end of the body. This setting releases oil at a pressure of 60 lb per sq in.

All models have an oil-pressure relief valve in the feed to the overhead rockers. It comprises a $\frac{3}{16}$ in. steel ball, a spring, and a plug screwed into the crankcase casting. The correct pressure is obtained when the plug is screwed right home. All new machines have their oil-pressure relief valves carefully adjusted by the makers, and this initial adjustment should not be disturbed.

Internal Oil Pipes. The pipes exposed when the crankcase near-side cover is removed should not normally be disturbed. If you do have occasion to remove the pipes, when replacing them make sure that the joint faces are absolutely clean and apply jointing compound sparingly so that it does not enter the oil passages.

DECARBONIZING AND VALVE GRINDING

Symptoms of Excessive Carbon Deposits. Carbon deposits gradually form on the piston crown and various parts of the combustion chamber. When carbon deposits become *excessive* the engine power output is considerably reduced, the exhaust note becomes rather "woolly," and there is a marked tendency for knocking or "pinking" (injurious to the engine bearings) when accelerating and hill climbing. The sparking plug also becomes very dirty quickly.

When Decarbonizing is Necessary. The symptoms just mentioned indicate that decarbonizing is necessary *immediately*. You should not continue to ride a motor-cycle which *definitely* needs decarbonizing, or damage may result. Usually decarbonizing is necessary after covering 2,500 miles on a *new* machine and subsequently about every 5,000 miles, unless the symptoms of excessive carbon deposits previously mentioned develop sooner or later. Do not decarbonize until this is *really necessary*. When removing the cylinder head for decarbonizing the head and piston, always remove both valves so that the ports in the cylinder head can be effectively cleaned and the valves ground-in where this is found necessary.

Is Cylinder Barrel Removal Necessary? It is not necessary each time the engine is decarbonized, but the barrel should be removed every *alternate* decarbonizing, or when there is loss of engine compression (not caused by bad valve-seating) suggesting that the piston rings need close inspection and possible renewal. When the cylinder barrel is removed the opportunity can be taken to examine closely the piston skirt, and the cylinder bore. A check can also be made to see if there is excessive play in the big-end bearing of the connecting-rod.

Initial Preparations. Always have available a new rocker-box cover joint-washer and a new copper and asbestos cylinder-head gasket. Also for valve-grinding purposes, a valve-spring compressor (*see* Fig. 41), a valve-grinding tool (*see* Fig. 41), and a tin of *medium grade* valve-grinding paste such as Richford's. If cylinder barrel and piston removal are intended, have available a new cylinder-barrel base washer, a Royal Enfield gudgeon-pin extractor tool (Part No. E.5477A) or a proprietary tool (*see* Fig. 38), a new pair of gudgeon-pin circlips, and a pair of snipe-nosed pliers for circlip fitting.

If the engine is very dirty externally, clean it with a rag and paraffin, and see that you have to hand a clean box or other receptacle in which to place engine parts as they are removed.

Remove the Petrol Tank. Prior to dismantling the engine for decarbonizing and grinding-in the valves the petrol tank should *always* be removed. Its removal is very simple. Turn off the petrol tap and remove the petrol pipe after unscrewing its union nuts at both ends. Then remove the nut and tap out the rubber-mounted bolt which secures the front end of the tank to the frame, and pull upwards the rear of the tank to release the clip holding the rear of the tank to the rubber sleeve surrounding the top tube of the frame. The foregoing instructions apply to all 1958–66 Royal Enfield 250 and 350 c.c. models except the 1965-6 "Continental G.T." model. On this sports model the fibre-glass petrol tank should be removed as described below.

First turn off the petrol tap and remove the petrol pipe after unscrewing

GENERAL MAINTENANCE 71

its union nuts at both ends. Next remove the elastic strap from the groove at the rear of the petrol tank. Then remove the two securing-bolts and rubber bushes from the bottom of the tank and withdraw the tank from the machine. When doing this be very careful not to damage the upper side of the tank by moving it against the rear of the steering head or telescopic front-forks. The tank being made of fibre-glass is easily damaged. To prevent the risk of damage being caused, it is wise to lay a piece of felt or cardboard over the top of the tank at its front end prior to removing it.

To Remove Cylinder Head and Overhead Rocker Assembly. After removing the petrol tank, proceed as follows—

1. Disconnect and remove the oil pipe connected between the crankcase and the cylinder head.
2. Disconnect the steady rod at the cylinder head.
3. Disconnect the sparking plug H.T. lead and remove the plug, using the box-spanner in the tool-kit. Examine the copper washer.
4. Remove the exhaust pipe.
5. Roll back the rubber connexion (where fitted) from the Amal carburettor air-intake to the air filter, and withdraw the carburettor from the cylinder-head studs after removing the two securing-nuts. Examine the joint washer. Tie up the carburettor in a convenient position with the air and throttle control-cables attached.
6. Referring to Fig. 35, remove the single nut (2) which secures the rocker-box cover (1) to the cylinder head and remove the cover. Also carefully remove the gasket (3). If not in perfect condition, renew it.
7. Turn the engine over slowly until the piston is at or near T.D.C. with both valves closed.
8. On *earlier type engines* remove the two-piece bearings for the overhead-rocker units (*see* Fig. 35), or on *later type engines* the one-piece housing for the two overhead-rocker spindles (*see* Fig. 36).

To remove each of the two-piece bearings provided on *earlier type engines*, referring to Fig. 35, remove the four $\frac{1}{4}$ in. nuts (5) and washers from the studs (9) securing the bearing halves (4) and the base plate (8). Then lift off the two bearing halves, complete with the overhead-rocker unit (6).

To remove the one-piece housing for the two overhead-rocker units on *later type engines*, referring to Fig. 36, remove the four $\frac{3}{16}$ in. nuts and washers (2) positioned at the ends of the housing (1). Also remove the single $\frac{3}{16}$ in. nut (3) located at the centre of the housing. The one-piece housing can then be lifted off the five studs (8), (10), together with the two overhead-rocker assemblies (4), (5).

9. After removing the two overhead-rocker bearings or the one-piece housing, withdraw the two push-rods.
10. Referring to Fig. 36, remove the four sleeve nuts (7) and washers from inside the rocker-box (6) and also remove the single plain nut (11) positioned near the sparking-plug hole. This applies to *all* engines.

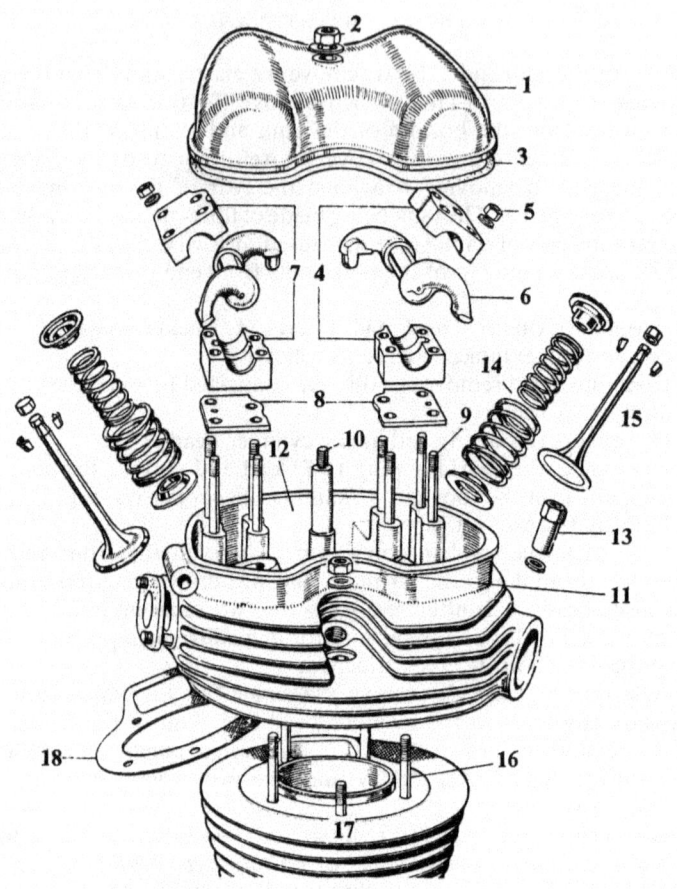

Fig. 35. Exploded View Showing Cylinder Barrel and Earlier Type Cylinder Head with Detachable Two-piece Overhead-rocker Bearings, Rockers, Valves, and Valve Springs Removed

Key to Fig. 35

1. Rocker-box cover
2. Rocker-box cover securing nut
3. Rocker-box cover gasket
4. Exhaust overhead-rocker bearing (two halves)
5. Nuts (four), for studs 9, securing 4 to bosses in rocker-box
6. Exhaust overhead-rocker unit
7. Inlet overhead-rocker bearing (two halves)
8. Plates beneath 4 and 7
9. Studs (eight) supporting separate overhead-rocker bearings 4, 7
10. Stud, for nut 2, securing rocker-box cover
11. Plain nut (one), for stud 17, securing cylinder head and barrel
12. Rocker-box
13. Sleeve nuts (four), for large studs 16, securing cylinder head and barrel
14. Duplex valve spring with top and bottom collars
15. Exhaust valve with hardened end-cap and split-collet
16. Long crankcase studs (four), for sleeve nuts 13, securing cylinder head and barrel
17. Short crankcase stud (one), for plain nut 11, securing cylinder barrel and head
18. Cylinder-head gasket (copper and asbestos)

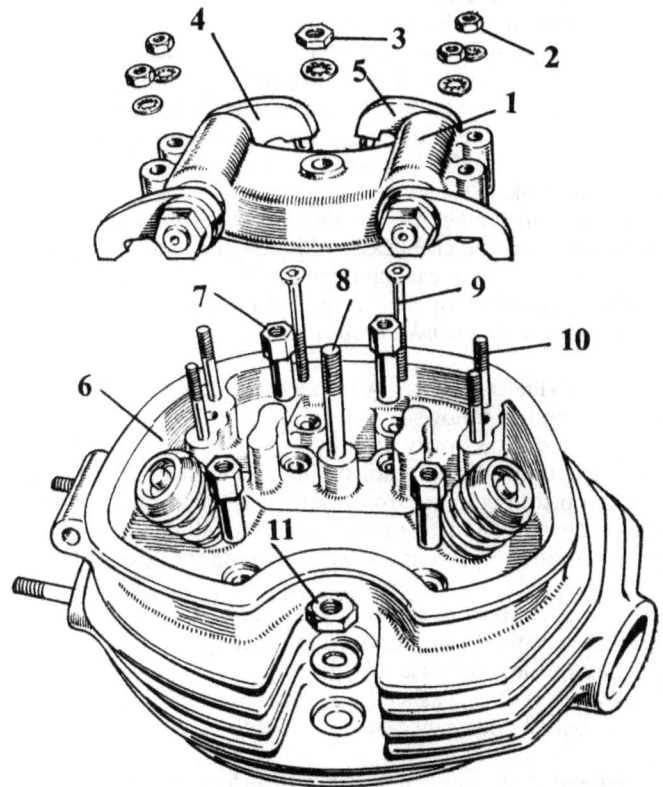

FIG. 36. EXPLODED VIEW OF LATER TYPE CYLINDER HEAD WITH ONE-PIECE OVERHEAD-ROCKER HOUSING REMOVED, AND WITH BOTH VALVES IN POSITION

The earlier type cylinder head is similar but has two separate overhead-rocker bearings as shown in Fig. 35, and only one Allen screw is provided instead of the two shown above at 9.

1. One-piece overhead-rocker housing
2. Nuts (four), for studs *10*, securing *1* to rocker-box bosses
3. Nut (one), for stud *8*, securing *1* to rocker-box *6*
4. Inlet overhead-rocker assembly
5. Exhaust overhead-rocker assembly
6. Rocker-box
7. Sleeve nuts (four), for long crankcase studs, securing cylinder head and cylinder barrel (*see* Fig. 35)
8. Stud, for nut *3*, securing *1* to *6*
9. Allen screws (two) for securing cylinder head to cylinder barrel
10. Studs (four), for nuts *2*, securing overhead-rocker housing *1*
11. Plain nut (one), for short crankcase stud, securing cylinder head and cylinder barrel (*see* Fig. 35)

(*The Enfield Cycle Co. Ltd.*)

On an earlier type engine with aluminium-alloy cylinder head also remove, in addition to the five head-securing nuts just mentioned, the single counter-sunk Allen screw located between the two sleeve nuts on the push-rod side of the cylinder head (not shown in Fig. 35).

On a later type engine with an aluminium-alloy cylinder head it is necessary to remove, in addition to the five sleeve nuts, the two Allen screws (9) located in the push-rod tunnel. These (see Fig. 36) are sometimes overlooked.

11. Lift the cylinder head from the five studs projecting through the cylinder barrel from the crankcase. Should the cylinder head be found difficult to remove, due to carbon deposits at its base, tap the head gently with a soft-nose hammer or mallet applied beneath the exhaust and inlet ports. *Do not tap the cylinder-head fins.*

To Remove Cylinder Barrel. After removing the cylinder head, remove the cylinder barrel as follows—

1. Rotate the engine slowly until the piston is at or near B.D.C.
2. Lift the cylinder barrel until its lower end clears the five crankcase studs and the piston emerges from the end of the cylinder bore. Steady the piston with one hand to prevent its skirt falling sharply against the connecting-rod and to prevent the latter striking the edge of the crankcase mouth.
3. To protect the piston, and to prevent dirt or foreign matter entering the crankcase, wrap a clean cloth around the connecting-rod and piston so that it blocks the crankcase mouth.
4. Remove the paper washer from the crankcase face and thoroughly clean up the barrel and crankcase joint-faces.

Removing and Replacing the Overhead Rockers. This is not necessary unless the plain bearings become worn after a very big mileage. Wear of the ends of the rockers which contact the valves can always be counteracted by adjusting the valve clearances.

On earlier type engines with the spindles of the overhead-rocker units located in detachable bearings, as shown at (4) and (7) in Fig. 35, the units can, of course, be removed merely by separating the bearing halves.

On later type engines with the overhead-rocker units in a one-piece rocker housing, as shown in Fig. 36, it is necessary to remove one nut from each rocker-arm spindle. Withdraw the washer and rocker arm from the spindle on the same side, and then from the opposite side pull out the other rocker arm together with the spindle.

When replacing the overhead rocker-arm units make sure that the rounded ends of the rockers are on the *push-rod side* (the near-side) of the rocker-box. Where detachable rocker bearings are fitted make sure that the oil feed holes in the bottom halves of the housings and in the plates beneath them (see Fig. 35) are unobstructed and register with each other and with the holes in the respective rocker-box bosses.

Where a one-piece overhead-rocker housing is provided, both the rockers are detachable from their spindles and to ensure correct assembly the following should be noted: the rocker on the push-rod side should be secured to the spindle by a plain washer and nut; the rocker on the valve side should have a double spring-washer positioned between the rocker bearing and the rocker.

Piston Removal. The piston fitted to all 1958 and later engines is of low-expansion aluminium alloy, heat-treated, and slightly oval. It has

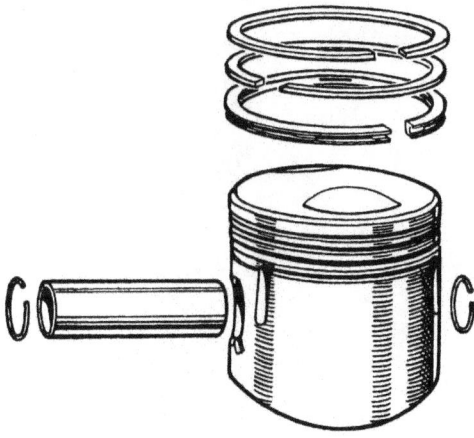

FIG. 37. SHOWING PISTON WITH ITS CIRCLIPS, GUDGEON-PIN, AND PISTON RINGS REMOVED

Note the slotted scraper-ring below the two compression rings. The top compression ring is chromium-plated

(*The Enfield Cycle Co. Ltd.*)

two compression rings (the top one chromium-plated) and one slotted scraper-ring (*see* Fig. 37).

Piston removal from the connecting-rod is not necessary for decarbonizing and if engine compression and engine performance are good the piston and piston rings should be left well alone. At 10,000 mile intervals, or every *alternate* decarbonizing, the cylinder barrel should, as mentioned on page 70, be removed and the piston and piston rings closely examined, and carbon deposits removed from inside the piston and from beneath the piston rings if new rings are required. Thorough inspection and cleaning necessitates the removal of the piston from the connecting-rod.

The piston is secured to the small-end bearing of the connecting-rod by a gudgeon-pin which is a tight fit in the piston bosses and has a circlip at each end to prevent end movement in these bosses. The removal of one or both, preferably both, circlips is necessary in order to remove the gudgeon-pin. Prior to removing the circlip(s) never omit to cover up the crankcase mouth with a large cloth to prevent a circlip dropping into the crankcase, a most disastrous occurrence. Circlip removal should be effected with a small electrical screwdriver or the tang end of a pointed file.

Where a motor-cycle has covered a considerable mileage it is sometimes possible to tap out the gudgeon-pin gently with a soft-nose hammer or a small mallet if the piston is first warmed by applying a cloth to it after

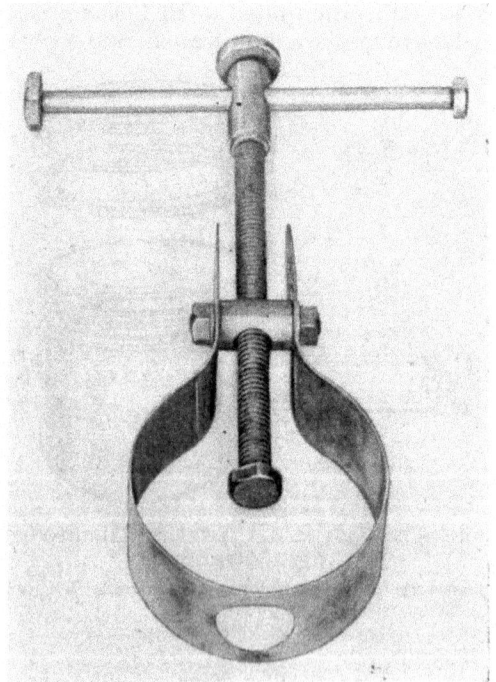

FIG. 38. A SUITABLE PROPRIETARY TOOL (THE TERRY) FOR REMOVING OR REPLACING A VERY TIGHT GUDGEON-PIN

The tool shown has three pads for fitting different size gudgeon-pins, but in the author's opinion the use of a Royal Enfield tool (Part No. 5477A) is preferable for Royal Enfield pistons

immersing the cloth in hot water and rinsing it out. The piston must be firmly supported on the opposite side when tapping out the gudgeon-pin. Usually it is necessary to draw out the gudgeon-pin with a Royal Enfield gudgeon-pin extractor (Part No. E.5477A) or else to press it out with a proprietary tool such as the Terry illustrated in Fig. 38. When using the Royal Enfield tool, position the extractor body so that it contacts the piston with its spindle passing through the gudgeon-pin. Then fit to the recess on the projecting end of the spindle the small collar provided, and turn the tommy-bar *anti-clockwise* until the gudgeon-pin is withdrawn. The use

GENERAL MAINTENANCE

of the Terry tool shown in Fig. 38 to press out the gudgeon-pin is self-obvious.

Before laying aside the gudgeon-pin, file a small nick on one end of the pin to indicate its original position in the piston and to ensure correct replacement. This is important, as is the replacement of the piston in its original position on the connecting-rod. This piston need not be marked (*see* page 84).

Examining and Removing Piston Rings. The two compression rings above the scraper-ring (*see* Fig. 39) are responsible for maintaining good

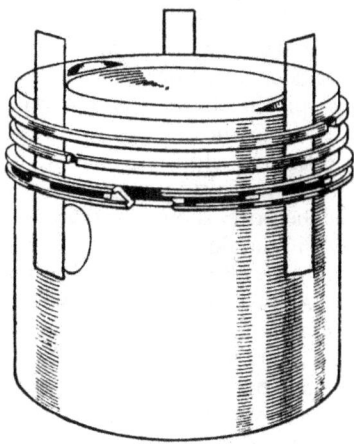

FIG. 39. THE SAFEST METHOD OF REMOVING AND FITTING THE PISTON RINGS

engine compression. They must therefore be full of spring, free in the piston-ring grooves, and set with their gaps positioned at 120 degrees to each other. If all three rings are bright all the way round, they are obviously being polished through being in full contact with the cylinder bore surface. In this case do not disturb them. If, on the other hand, they are discoloured at some points, they are not in full contact with the cylinder bore surface, and ignited fuel blows past them. Sometimes piston rings become stuck in their grooves with burnt oil and carbon deposits and will function satisfactorily only after cleaning the piston-ring grooves. Where piston-ring gaps are excessive, the rings are scored, have lost their springiness, are vertically loose in their grooves, or have brown patches, remove the rings and fit new ones.

Piston rings, especially scraper-rings, are easily broken, being made of cast-iron and of very small section. They cannot safely be opened out wider than will permit them to slip over the piston crown. For this reason when removing piston rings it is advisable to insert three small strips of metal (about ⅜ in. wide and 2 in. long) between the rings and the piston as shown in Fig. 39. Be careful when replacing old rings or fitting new rings (*see* page 79) to fit them correctly. Before fitting new rings, thoroughly clean (*see* page 79) the piston-ring grooves, because carbon deposits force the rings out and make new rings too tight a fit in the cylinder bore. If it is decided not to fit new rings it is generally advisable *not* to remove slight carbon deposits from the backs of the rings and from the ring grooves unless the rings have become stuck. Stuck rings can usually be freed with paraffin.

When piston ring renewal is called for, always fit rings supplied by The Enfield Cycle Co. Ltd., or one of their approved dealers. Piston rings are made to extremely fine limits. On new pistons the two compression rings have a side clearance of 0·003 in.–0·005 in. in the piston-ring grooves. The scraper-ring has a side clearance of 0·002 in.–0·004 in. Do not attempt to fit oversize piston rings to compensate for wear unless an oversize piston and a rebore are necessary. Pistons 0·020 in. and 0·040 in. oversize, with similar oversize piston rings to suit, are obtainable.

The correct gap for all *new* piston rings, checked in an unworn part (the bottom or top) of the bore, should be 0·015 in.–0·020 in., except on the "350 Bullet" where it should be 0·011 in.–0·015 in. It is advisable after removing a piston to check the gaps of all three piston rings, using a suitable feeler gauge. Always renew a ring where its gap is found to exceed $\frac{1}{16}$ in. If new standard or oversize rings are fitted, check their gaps before fitting them to the piston. When checking the gaps, insert each piston ring into an unworn part of the cylinder bore and afterwards slide up the piston so that its crown contacts and squares up the ring.

Examine the ends of each ring. If they are bright, the ring gap is too small; if heavily coated with carbon, the gap is probably too big. Should the gap of a new ring be too small, clamp the ring between two wooden blocks in a vice and file *one* of the diagonal ends *slightly*. If a new ring is excessively tight in its groove, rub down one side of the ring on a sheet of carborundum paper laid flat on a piece of plate glass or a surface plate.

Decarbonizing the Cylinder Head. Always decarbonize thoroughly because carbon forms less readily on smooth surfaces. With a proprietary scraper or a blunt screwdriver remove all carbon deposits from the combustion chamber. To avoid damaging the valve seats in the head after removing the valves (*see* page 80), re-insert the valves in their guides.

Remove all traces of carbon from the interior surfaces and do not forget the sparking-plug hole and the exhaust port. If a curved rifler is used to clean up the ports, be particularly careful not to allow the pointed end of the rifler to scratch the valve seats. Never use emery-cloth or any other abrasive to clean and polish the combustion chamber of an aluminium-alloy cylinder head, and *in no circumstances* attempt to remove carbon by immersing this type of head in a hot caustic-soda or potash solution. Most disastrous results are inevitable.

Decarbonizing the Piston. Be careful when removing carbon deposits from the comparatively soft aluminium-alloy piston. *Do not use emery-cloth*, only a blunt screwdriver or a proprietary scraper. Never attempt to remove carbon from the lands between the piston rings or from the piston skirt. A little carbon is often formed on the inside of the piston, and where the piston is removed this should be carefully scraped off. When using a screwdriver to remove internal deposits avoid allowing the screwdriver shank to bump against the piston skirt.

Where carbon deposits in the piston-ring grooves are very considerable, and always prior to fitting new rings, scrape off all deposits with a piece of broken piston ring inserted into a wooden handle and ground to a vee as shown in Fig. 40. Alternatively use a proprietary scraper. If used piston

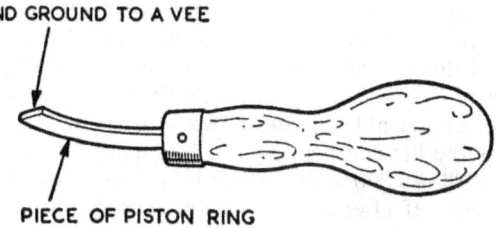

FIG. 40. A HOME-MADE TOOL FOR CLEANING PISTON-RING GROOVES

rings are in satisfactory condition, do not, as previously mentioned on page 78, remove *slight* carbon deposits from the piston-ring grooves and from the backs of the rings.

After thoroughly decarbonizing the piston, wash it thoroughly in clean paraffin and replace the three used rings, or fit new ones.

Fitting the Piston Rings. To avoid breaking the rings when fitting them to the piston it is desirable to use the method shown in Fig. 39. It is of extreme importance to fit the piston rings the right way up and in the correct grooves. Fit the chromium-plated compression ring into the top groove with the word "TOP" uppermost; fit the taper-faced compression ring into the centre groove, also with the word "TOP" uppermost; where a one-piece scraper-ring is provided, fit it either way up, but where a split-type scraper ring is used fit it into the bottom groove so that that part of the ring having projections is at the top.

Cleaning the Silencer. The silencer fitted to all later models except the "250 Clipper" should be dismantled for cleaning when decarbonizing the cylinder head and piston. To dismantle the silencer, remove the $\frac{5}{16}$ in. nut and tab-washer in its tail and withdraw the tail-piece and central body from the long central stud positioned in the front portion of the silencer.

Testing Small- and Big-end Bearings for Wear. With the piston removed, the opportunity can be taken of testing the small- and big-end bearings for wear. The fully-floating gudgeon-pin should be a free working fit in the connecting-rod small-end bearing, and a rather tight fit in the piston bosses. Insert the gudgeon-pin in the small-end and check for any "rock" in the bearing. No appreciable "rock" is permissible. The small-end bearing is not a separate bush but is a hole bored in the Hiduminium RR 56 light-alloy connecting-rod, and a large diameter gudgeon-pin is fitted to reduce wear to the minimum. If after a very big mileage considerable play develops in the small-end bearing, the eye of the connecting-rod can be further bored out to receive a bronze bush, but this repair is rarely necessary if the engine is regularly decarbonized and the motor-cycle is handled with care.

To test the big-end bearing for excessive wear, with the connecting-rod at B.D.C., grip the rod firmly with both hands and attempt to push-and-pull it up and down, preferably with the big-end oil film dispersed. A slight degree of "shake" and some side float are permissible, but there should be no appreciable up-and-down movement. Under favourable circumstances the big-end bearing can be expected to remain serviceable for up to 30,000–40,000 miles, though it is impossible to specify any definite mileage. If after a big mileage appreciable up-and-down play can be felt in the small-end, the big-end, or the crankshaft main bearings, the engine should be removed from the frame for new parts to be fitted by The Enfield Cycle Co. Ltd. or one of their authorized repair specialists. You should not tackle this job yourself. On 250 c.c. engines the light-alloy connecting-rod has a detachable big-end bearing cap secured by two high-tensile steel bolts, and the bearing itself comprises two white-metalled steel liners which are renewable. 350 c.c. engines have a one-piece light-alloy connecting-rod with a replaceable plain big-end bearing bush.

To Remove Both Valves. As has been mentioned on page 70, each time the cylinder head is removed for decarbonizing it is advisable to remove both valves in order that the valve ports can be cleaned thoroughly and so that the valves and their seats can be inspected and the valves, *if necessary*, ground-in. Valve removal entails, of course, the preliminary removal of the two-piece overhead-rocker bearings or the one-piece overhead-rocker bearing housing fitted to earlier and later engines respectively. This should preferably be done during cylinder head removal as described on page 71. On all later type engines with the bearing housing shown in Fig. 36 it *must* be done during head removal, otherwise the head cannot be removed.

The valve and duplex valve-spring arrangement provided on all engines is shown in Fig. 35. Note that on the "Crusader Sports" and all later engines no hardened valve stem-end caps are fitted and the top valve-spring collar is secured to the valve stem by a split-collet which has a narrow internal projection fitting into a corresponding groove in the valve stem.

GENERAL MAINTENANCE

The inlet and exhaust valves are *not interchangeable*, having different size stems and being made of different grade steel.

Where hardened valve-stem end caps are fitted, remove these prior to removing the valves from the cylinder head. Sometimes an end cap becomes stuck on the end of the valve stem, especially where an exhaust valve is concerned. To remove, prise it off with a screwdriver, or alternatively grip the end cap in a vice and pull the cylinder head away. Remove each valve in the following manner.

Place the forked end of a suitable screw type valve-spring compressor (*see* Fig. 41) squarely on the valve-spring top collar and the pointed end

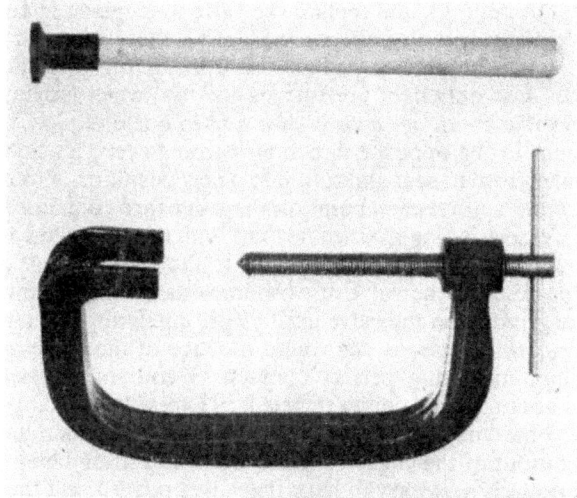

FIG. 41. SUITABLE PROPRIETARY TOOLS FOR (BELOW) COMPRESSING VALVE SPRINGS AND (ABOVE) FOR GRINDING-IN VALVES

Royal Enfield spares stockists supply a Terry valve-spring compressor (Part No. TE/1124) and a valve-grinding tool (Part No. TE/1167) consisting of a valve-stem holder instead of the suction-type tool illustrated. Where a valve holder is used, the valves, have, of course, to be pulled up against their seats while grinding-in

of the screw in the centre of the valve head. Then turn the screw clockwise until the duplex valve-spring is compressed sufficiently to enable the split-collet to be removed from the valve stem. If the split-collet refuses to come away, deliver a sharp tap on the forked end of the valve-spring compressor. Avoid compressing the duplex valve-spring excessively. After removing the split-collet withdraw the duplex valve-spring and its top collar. Then pull the inlet or exhaust valve from its guide in the cylinder head. If the valve does not come away readily, remove any slight burrs with a carborundum slip from the end of the valve stem, otherwise there is a possibility of the valve guide being damaged when removing the valve. The bottom valve-spring collar can be left in position. After removing both valves, keep the top collars, split-collets, and valve springs paired up with the corresponding inlet and exhaust valves.

Grinding-in the Valves. Examine closely the inlet and exhaust valve seats and valve faces. Where pitting of a valve seat and/or face exists, the valve concerned must be ground-in, using the following procedure after thoroughly cleaning the face of the valve and its seat in the cylinder head.

With a piece of rag or a finger-tip smear the face of the valve with a thin film of *medium* grinding paste (coarse at first if dealing with a valve and seat in very poor condition), and replace the valve in its guide. Then grind-in the valve, preferably with a suction-type of tool (*see* Fig. 41). It is advisable to moisten the rubber pad of this tool before applying it to the valve head. Use only light pressure on the tool when moving the valve. Rotate the valve about *one quarter of a turn* in one direction, and then an equal amount in the opposite direction, pausing every few oscillations to raise the valve from its seat and turn it to a new position. Gradually work the valve round so that each point on the valve face contacts each part of the seat. Cease grinding-in when no "cut" can be felt and the valve begins to "sing," and apply more grinding paste to the bevelled edge of the valve face, if after cleaning the valve in paraffin, some pitting is still visible.

Continue grinding-in the valve until *all* pitting disappears and there is a perfectly *smooth and bright ring* round the face of the valve and also the valve seating, indicating perfect contact. Depth of contact does not matter and about $\frac{1}{32}$ in. is quite sufficient. Excessive grinding-in causes a valve to become "pocketed" and this can cause a considerable decline in the power output of the engine. In the event of pitting being very extensive and deep, it is necessary to have the valves refaced and the seats recut by a Royal Enfield repair specialist or by the manufacturers.

After grinding-in a valve be sure to remove *every trace* of grinding paste from the valve and its seat. Absolutely no trace of abrasive must be left. Insert each valve in its seat and check for wear in its guide. Excessive clearance between the valve stem and guide necessitates renewal of the valve guide, followed by re-cutting of the valve seat to the correct profile. Valve guide renewal is very seldom required and where necessary is best undertaken by a Royal Enfield repair specialist or the manufacturers. Often a valve stem wears more than its guide and a distinct shoulder is felt near the neck of the valve. In this case the renewal of the valve (which must be ground-in) usually remedies slackness between the valve and guide without a new guide having to be fitted.

Are the Valve Springs Weak? To decide whether they are, it is necessary to check their free length. This can be done by comparing their length with the length of new springs or by measuring their actual length. Loss of valve-spring tension due to heat sometimes occurs after running several thousands of miles, and this reduces engine efficiency. Renew valve springs when their free length is $\frac{1}{8}$ in. less than that of new springs.

The free length of new duplex springs is as follows—"Crusader 250" and "250 Clipper": $2\frac{1}{32}$ in. for inner and outer springs; "Crusader Sports," "Crusader Super 5," "Continental," "Continental G.T.," and "350 Bullet": $1\frac{1}{2}$ in. for inner spring and $1\frac{11}{16}$ in. for outer spring.

Replacing the Valves. After the inlet and exhaust valves have been satisfactorily ground-in, replace each valve in the following manner. Smear the valve stem with some engine oil and replace the valve in the correct cylinder-head guide. Next replace the inner and outer valve spring, followed by the top collar. It is assumed that the bottom collar has been left in position. Be careful not to interchange the inlet and exhaust components.

With a screw type valve-spring compressor such as that shown in Fig. 41, compress the duplex valve-spring sufficiently to enable the split-collet to be fitted to the groove near the end of the valve stem. Make sure that the split-collet beds down properly on the valve stem groove and in the top collar. The application of a little grease to the inside of a split-collet will help it to stick on the valve stem until the pressure on the duplex spring is released. After releasing the pressure hold a box-spanner over the top collar and tap it sharply. This should ensure that the split-collet beds down properly. Proper bedding down is imperative because if a split-collet comes adrift with the engine running, the valve is likely to drop, smash up the piston, and do other serious damage. Finally replace the two hardened valve-stem end caps where originally fitted.

After Replacing Both Valves. It is a good plan to test the valve seatings by pouring some petrol into the ports and watching for leakage past the valves. Petrol should not creep past the valves until a considerable time has elapsed. If it does, this is sure evidence that the valves have not been sufficiently ground-in, and the remedy is to remove the valves and continue grinding-in. Where reasonable care is taken when grinding-in the valves, this test is, of course, not necessary and good engine compression is assured, provided that the piston rings are also in good condition, and the cylinder bore not excessively worn.

Fitting the Piston to the Connecting-rod. If both gudgeon-pin circlips have been removed, fit a *new* circlip into one of the piston-boss annular grooves, using if necessary a pair of small snipe-nose pliers. Make sure that the circlip beds down properly and is fully expanded, remembering that a loose circlip can come adrift and ruin the cylinder bore. If the gudgeon-pin is a *moderately tight* fit in the piston bosses, it is a good plan to warm up the piston as mentioned on page 76 before fitting it to the small-end of the connecting-rod. Before replacing the piston, fit the piston rings (*see* page 79) correctly and see that the mouth of the crankcase is covered with a cloth. Position the piston bosses against the small-end bearing with the piston the correct way round. If the piston has a split skirt the split must face towards the *front* of the engine. Most Royal Enfield pistons are marked in the vicinity of the exhaust-valve depression with the word "FRONT" to ensure correct replacement.

Start inserting the gudgeon-pin into the piston-boss hole opposite to where the circlip has been fitted. Before inserting it make sure that it is the correct way round (*see* page 77) and smear it liberally with some clean engine oil. Then gently tap the pin in, holding the piston firmly on the opposite side when using a soft-nose hammer or small mallet. Never use excessive force. If the gudgeon-pin is a *very tight* fit (it usually is), *always* press the pin in, using the Royal Enfield tool referred to on page 76 or else a proprietary tool such as that illustrated in Fig. 38. As soon as the end of the gudgeon-pin contacts the circlip already fitted, fit a *new* circlip on the other side. Make sure that it beds down properly and is fully expanded.

To Replace the Cylinder Barrel. The following is the correct procedure—

1. See that the joint faces of the cylinder barrel and the crankcase are absolutely clean and fit a new cylinder-base paper washer to the crankcase face, after smearing it lightly with some jointing compound. Red Hermatite is recommended.

2. Rotate the engine slowly so that the piston is just past B.D.C.

3. Smear the piston (especially the piston rings) and the cylinder bore with some clean engine oil, and space the piston-ring gaps so that they are at 120 degrees to each other. Where a split-skirt piston is fitted, make sure that no piston-ring gap is in the immediate vicinity of the split in the piston skirt.

4. Holding the cylinder barrel vertically over the five crankcase studs and piston with one hand, with the other offer up the piston to the cylinder-barrel bore. Should you experience some difficulty in holding the piston and cylinder barrel steady, it is advisable to obtain assistance or else to tie up the barrel to the frame top-tube with some stout string. Keep the barrel and piston absolutely square to each other and squeeze the piston rings by hand or with a proprietary metal strap (without disturbing the ring-gap position) as the piston slowly enters the cylinder bore. Do not use strong pressure if a ring sticks, otherwise the ring will break.

5. When the cylinder barrel has bedded right down on to the cylinder-base washer, turn the engine over slowly to make sure that the piston moves freely in the bore. If you do not replace the cylinder head immediately, cover up the top of the cylinder barrel and piston.

To Replace Cylinder Head and Overhead-rocker Assembly. Do this in the following manner—

1. Check that the joint faces of the cylinder head and the cylinder barrel are absolutely clean, and fit a new copper-and-asbestos gasket over the

cylinder barrel spigot. Before fitting this gasket (shown at (*18*) in Fig. 35) smear both its faces with a thin film of joining compound, such as red Hermatite.

2. Rotate the engine until the piston is at T.D.C.

3. Replace the cylinder head, with both valves fitted, over the five crankcase studs and lower it until it rests on the cylinder-head gasket.

4. Referring to Fig. 36, replace, with their washers, the four sleeve nuts (*7*) and the single plain nut (*11*) which secure the cylinder head and barrel to the crankcase. Tighten all five nuts evenly, firmly, and in a diagonal order to prevent any risk of head distortion. Also on an *earlier type engine* with an aluminium-alloy cylinder head, replace and tighten the single Allen-screw. This must be inserted between the two sleeve nuts on the near-side. On a *later type engine* with an aluminium-alloy cylinder head, replace and tighten the two Allen-screws shown at (*9*) in Fig. 36. These screws require insertion in the push-rod tunnel.

5. Replace the inlet and exhaust push-rods correctly. Their adjustable cups must, of course, be located at the top and the inlet push-rod (the longer one) must pass through the *outer* of the two holes in the base of the cylinder barrel. It is desirable to oil both ends of the push-rods before inserting them through the push-rod tunnel into the cups on the cam followers.

6. Referring to Fig. 35, on an *earlier type engine* with two-piece bearings for the overhead rockers, fit each assembly in the following manner, being careful not to interchange any of the inlet and exhaust components. Dealing with the exhaust assembly, replace plate (*8*), if previously removed, over the four studs (*9*) with the oil hole to the front. Next fit the bottom half of the rocker bearing (*4*) over the plate, making sure that its oil hole at the bottom registers with the oil hole in the plate. Then replace the exhaust overhead-rocker unit (*6*) which should be oiled. Fit the top half of the bearing over the studs and exhaust rocker shaft; see that the whole assembly beds down. A light tap with a hammer will ensure this. The top and bottom halves of the bearing must be in true alignment, and the rounded end of the rocker must, of course, be on the near-side so that it can later be engaged with the exhaust push-rod. Fit to the studs (*9*) the four $\frac{1}{4}$-in. nuts and washers (*5*) and tighten all four nuts evenly and in a diagonal order. After tightening down the nuts check that the rocker unit (*6*) moves freely.

7. Referring to Fig. 36, on a *later type engine* with a one-piece housing for the overhead rockers, fit the housing complete with the overhead rockers as follows. Position the housing over the five studs (*8*), (*10*). Make sure that it is squarely home over the studs and rests on the rocker-box bosses. A light tap with a hammer will ensure this. Then replace the single $\frac{5}{16}$ in. nut and washer (*3*) on the central stud (*8*) and the four $\frac{3}{16}$-in. nuts and washers (*2*) on the corner studs (*10*). Tighten down all five nuts evenly and in a diagonal order.

8. With the piston still at T.D.C. engage the cups (which should be

adjusted to be low down) of the inlet and exhaust push-rods with the ball ends of the inlet and exhaust overhead-rockers respectively. The correct assembly of the push-rods is shown in Fig. 44. The inlet push-rod is *slightly longer* than the exhaust push-rod and is actuated by the *outer* cam follower. Make absolutely sure that the push-rods are properly engaged with the cam-follower cups.

9. Adjust the valve clearances as described on page 63.

10. Referring to Fig. 35, fit a new gasket (*3*) for the rocker-box cover and replace the cover (*1*). Before fitting the gasket smear it with a little jointing compound such as red Hermatite. If your engine has a pronounced tendency for oil leakage to occur from the rocker-box cover-joint it is advisable to fit *two gaskets* instead of one. Their combined thickness compensates for joint-face irregularities. Tighten the cover nut (*2*) securely and do not omit the washer.

11. After fitting a new joint-washer if necessary, position the Amal "monobloc" carburettor over the two cylinder-head studs and firmly secure the carburettor flange to the cylinder head by means of the two nuts. Tighten these nuts evenly to prevent distorting the carburettor flange. If your tool-box contains an air filter, re-connect the rubber connexion at the carburettor air-intake.

12. Re-position the exhaust system so that the end of the exhaust pipe goes fully home into the exhaust port.

13. Connect up the oil feed-pipe from the crankcase to the rocker-box. Before replacing the pipe it is a good plan to blow through it to make sure that it is unobstructed. Prior to tightening the union nut at the bottom end of the oil pipe, check that the crankcase union is securely tightened. Replace the washers behind the banjos when securing the upper end of the oil pipe to the rocker-box and tighten the banjo bolts *firmly*, not forgetting to replace the two outer washers. To avoid the risk of damaging the oil pipe when firmly tightening the banjo bolts it is a good plan to hold each banjo still by slipping over it an open-ended spanner.

14. Connect the end of the steady rod to the cylinder head. The nut must be firmly tightened.

15. Kick the engine over smartly several times to ensure that everything is in order and to provide some oil circulation.

16. Replace the sparking plug and its copper washer. With a box-spanner tighten it securely. Renew the washer if not perfect. It is assumed that the sparking plug is of the correct type, is clean, and correctly gapped (*see* pages 49, 50).

After Engine Assembly is Complete. Replace the petrol tank and on all machines, except the 1965-6 "Continental G.T." model, secure it firmly by means of the rubber-mounted bolt and nut at the front end and the clip securing the rear end to the rubber sleeve surrounding the top tube of the frame. Then re-connect the petrol pipe to the tank and carburettor float-chamber, tightening the union nuts securely.

GENERAL MAINTENANCE 87

On the 1965-6 "Continental G.T." model carefully position the petrol tank after laying a piece of felt or carboard over the top of the tank at its front end so as to avoid the possibility of damaging the fibreglass. Next replace the two rubber bushes (one on each side of the bottom bracket) and insert and tighten the two tank-securing bolts. Then replace the elastic strap over the groove at the rear of the tank. Should this strap become damaged, renew it immediately. Finally reconnect the petrol pipe to the tank and carburettor float-chamber. Tighten the two union nuts securely. When doing this it is advisable, especially in the case of the tank union, to use *two* spanners. The application of excessive pressure on the joint between the petrol tap and tank can cause damage which results in leakage.

After replacing the petrol pipe and tank, start up the engine and take the machine for a short trip. It should behave well. On your return, with the engine quite *hot*, remove the rocker-box cover and check all cylinder-head securing nuts for tightness. If there is any slackness, tighten the nuts concerned. After the engine has cooled right down, again check the valve clearances (*see* page 62).

IGNITION AND VALVE TIMING

The Camshaft and Contact-breaker-cam Drives. Referring to Fig. 42, the camshaft sprocket (*6*) is driven by a duplex chain from the timing sprocket on the near-side flywheel mainshaft (*see* Figs. 32, 44) and rotates the camshaft (*2*), actuating the valves, at *half engine speed*. Secured to the camshaft and positioned behind the cam-housing cover (shown at (*11*) in Fig. 32) is the camshaft pinion (*5*). This pinion drives the oil-pump spindle (*10*) via its pinion (*8*) and the idler pinion (*11*) at the same speed as the camshaft, and the contact-breaker cam (not shown) on the opposite end of the pump spindle therefore also rotates at half engine speed.

The Timing Marks. From the above it is clear that the correct valve timing is determined by the position of the timing sprocket teeth relative to the camshaft-sprocket teeth. A dash system of tooth marking (*see* Fig. 32) is used to ensure that the two sprockets are aligned so that the valve timing is correct. Obviously there must be no slackness in the duplex timing chain shown at (*1*) in Fig. 32.

Referring to Fig. 42, the three pinions (*5*), (*11*), (*8*) which drive the contact-breaker cam (not shown) on the pump spindle (*10*) have a dot system of tooth marking to ensure their relative positioning so that the contact-breaker cam opens the contact-breaker contacts just before the piston reaches T.D.C. on the compression stroke. The precise moment of the "break" can be set by re-timing the ignition as described on page 56. Only a minor adjustment is usually required. For obvious reasons slackness of the timing chain can adversely affect the ignition timing as well as the valve timing. Chain slackness can be taken up as described on page 64.

To Maintain Correct Ignition and Valve Timing. Summing up, provided that the timing and camshaft sprockets are assembled with the teeth dash marks aligned as shown in Fig. 32, and provided that the three pinions shown in Fig. 42 are assembled with the dot marks on their teeth registering

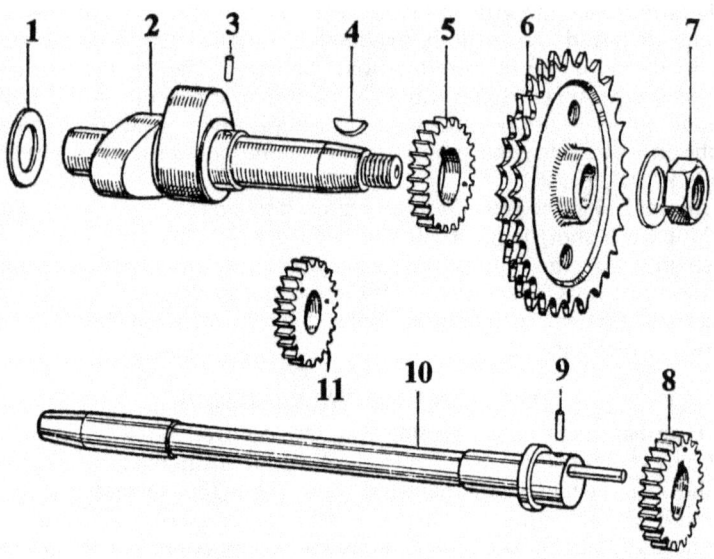

FIG. 42. SHOWING THE CAMSHAFT WITH ITS CHAIN-DRIVEN SPROCKET, AND THE OIL PUMP AND CONTACT-BREAKER SPINDLE WITH ITS THREE DRIVING PINIONS

1. Camshaft thrust-washer
2. Camshaft (exhaust cam)
3. Camshaft-pinion dowel
4. Camshaft-sprocket key
5. Camshaft pinion (with one dot mark)
6. Camshaft sprocket (with one dash mark)
7. Nut securing 6 to camshaft
8. Pinion for spindle *10* (with one dot mark)
9. Dowel for *8*
10. Oil pump and contact-breaker spindle (contact-breaker cam not shown)
11. Idler pinion (with two dot marks)

(*The Enfield Cycle Co. Ltd.*)

with dot marks on the teeth of adjacent pinions, no appreciable alteration in the ignition or valve timing is ever likely to occur.

To ensure precise valve timing check and if necessary adjust the valve clearances every 1,000 miles (*see* page 63) and every 2,000 miles check and if necessary adjust the tension of the timing chain (*see* page 64). To maintain precise ignition timing, check and if necessary adjust the contact-breaker gap every 6,000 miles. After a big mileage wear of the contacts and the rocker arm may necessitate re-timing by means of the contact carrier-plate or the contact-breaker cam as described on page 58. Never attempt to improve on the Royal Enfield ignition and valve timings.

GENERAL MAINTENANCE 89

DISMANTLING AND REPLACING THE CAM GEAR

To Dismantle. First remove the crankcase near-side cover (*see* page 32). Next remove the camshaft sprocket, the timing sprocket and the duplex timing chain (*see* page 66). Also remove the five ¼ in. nuts and washers which secure the cam-housing cover shown at (*11*) in Fig. 32. Withdraw the cam-housing cover. Then remove the camshaft, the cam followers, and the idler pinion shown at (*11*) in Fig. 42.

To Replace. See that the washers on the cam-follower spindle are replaced in this order: (*a*) thrust washer, (*b*) exhaust cam-follower, (*c*) spring washer, (*d*) inlet cam-follower, (*e*) thrust washer. The correct sequence is shown in Fig. 43. Note that the exhaust cam-follower is

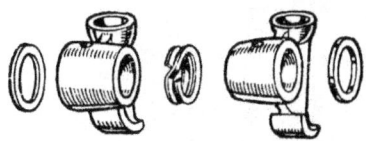

FIG. 43. THE CORRECT CAM-FOLLOWER ASSEMBLY ORDER
The exhaust cam-follower (right) is longer than the inlet one and should be replaced first
(*The Enfield Cycle Co. Ltd.*)

longer than the inlet cam-follower. When replacing the camshaft be sure to replace the 0·030 in. thrust washer which goes at the back of the camshaft adjacent to the crankcase.

Engage the pump, idler, and camshaft pinions so that their dot marks are opposite to one another. Note that because the idler pinion has one tooth less than the camshaft and pump pinions, the marks will only come opposite to each other every 23 revolutions, but this does not affect the timing once it is set. (*See* Fig. 42.)

On replacing the cam-housing cover make sure that the faces of the housing and cover are clean and use jointing compound with care. Before replacing the cam-housing cover the oil pump must be dismantled (*see* page 68) in order to fit the pump plungers over the peg on the pump spindle correctly.

MAJOR ENGINE OVERHAUL

After running 35,000 miles or more, according to how the engine has been used and maintained, the engine usually begins to run somewhat roughly and during decarbonizing a check for big-end wear (*see* page 80) reveals considerable "shake" in the big-end and mainshaft bearings. There may also be considerable loss of compression and power output due to a worn cylinder-bore. This indicates that a major engine overhaul, involving bearing renewal, has become necessary.

The average motor-cyclist has not the time, mechanical skill, or facilities for tackling this highly skilled work, and it is best to ride or despatch the

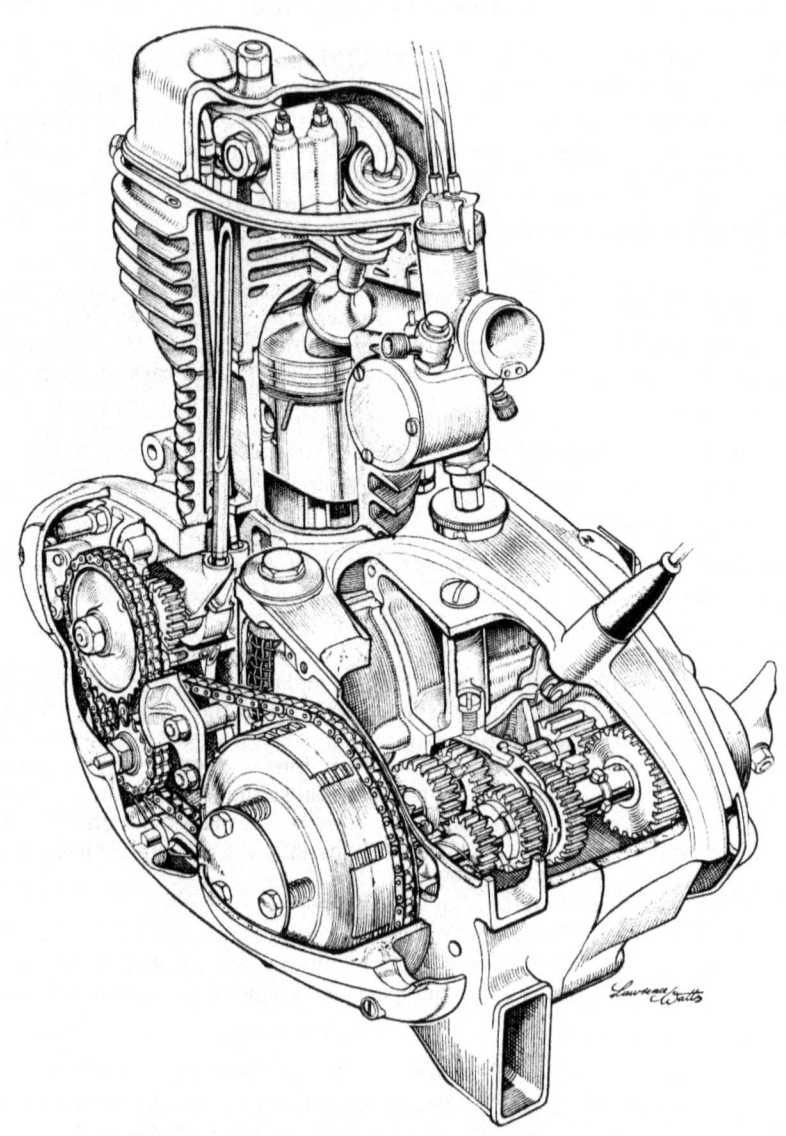

Fig. 44. Cut-away View of "Crusader" Power Unit Showing Engine Primary Transmission, and Gearbox Details

(*By courtesy of "Motor Cycle," London*)

machine to The Enfield Cycle Co. Ltd. of Redditch (phone: Redditch 121) or to an authorized firm which handles Royal Enfield repairs and has the necessary tools. Alternatively, remove the engine-gearbox unit from the frame (*see* below) and forward this to the makers or to an authorized repairer. Those who feel competent to undertake major overhaul, involving splitting the crankcase and renewing bearings, and have the necessary facilities (including some special Royal Enfield tools) should obtain a copy of the excellent *Royal Enfield Workshop Maintenance Manual* to obtain the necessary technical information.

Removing the Engine-gearbox Unit. To remove the unit from the frame the following is briefly the procedure required—
1. Disconnect the positive and negative leads from the battery.
2. Remove the petrol tank and its pipe (*see* page 70).
3. Disconnect the engine steady and the exhaust pipe.
4. Remove the secondary chain (*see* page 97).
5. Remove the Amal "monobloc" carburettor from the cylinder head.
6. Disconnect the alternator leads at the junction plugs.
7. Detach the contact-breaker lead from the ignition coil.
8. Disconnect the clutch cable from the handlebar lever.
9. Disconnect the H.T. lead from the sparking plug terminal.
10. Remove the footrests and their bar.
11. Where fitted, remove the rev.-counter drive from the crankcase near-side cover.
12. Remove the bolt and distance-piece securing the rear of the crankcase.
13. Support the engine on a suitable box or block.
14. Remove the engine rear-plates, complete with the centre stand, after removing the two $\frac{3}{8}$ in. bolts.
15. Remove the front engine plates.
16. Lift the engine-gearbox unit right out of the frame from the off-side.

THE GEARBOX

Foot Gear-change Adjustment. On all Royal Enfields the foot gear-change lever is mounted on a serrated shaft and its angle can be varied to suit different footrest positions. To make an adjustment, loosen the clamping screw, remove the gear-change lever, and replace it on the serrations which provide the most comfortable gear changing.

Gearbox Maintenance. Provided that you take reasonable care when gear changing, top-up the gearbox regularly about every 500 miles to the correct level, and drain and refill it every 5,000 miles (*see* page 34), you will find that the gearbox gives long and trouble-free service. An excellent feature of the Royal Enfield four- or five-speed gearbox is that the gears are actuated by a single striking fork. This makes it quite impossible to engage two gears simultaneously even if some wear has occurred.

92   THE SECOND BOOK OF THE ROYAL ENFIELD

Overhaul. Overhaul of the gearbox (*see* Fig. 44) should not be necessary until a very big mileage has been covered. Should it eventually become noisy and gear changing difficult it is advisable, unless you are a competent mechanic, to have the gearbox dismantled and very thoroughly overhauled by The Enfield Cycle Co. Ltd., or by an authorized or reputable repairer. If you have the necessary skill and facilities available for gearbox overhaul, read the appropriate instructions given in the maker's *Workshop Maintenance Manual*, a most helpful publication.

THE CLUTCH

To Prevent Clutch Slip. It is essential always to keep the clutch control correctly adjusted. *The clutch springs are not adjustable for tension.* Always maintain sufficient free movement (about $\frac{1}{16}$ in.) of the cable at the handlebar lever, otherwise the friction-insert plates (*see* Fig. 46) of the multi-plate clutch will not be pressed firmly against the metal driven-plates when the clutch is engaged, with the result that clutch slip damages or ruins the inserts.   If clutch slip occurs in spite of there being slackness in the clutch-control cable, remove and examine the clutch plates for wear of the cork or fabric inserts.   After a very big mileage renewal of the three (six on early "Crusader" models) springs may become necessary. The springs are, of course, subjected to considerable heat.

On a new Royal Enfield, or where the clutch driving-plates have had new friction-inserts fitted, some initial bedding-down of the inserts usually occurs, and an adjustment of the clutch control may be necessary after covering about 250 miles.   Subsequently an adjustment should only be required at intervals of about 1,000 miles.   But make an adjustment whenever free movement of the cable disappears.

To Adjust the Clutch Control. If bedding-down or wear of the cork or fabric inserts necessitates an adjustment being made, the following is the correct procedure.   Referring to Fig. 45, first slide back the plastic cover where the clutch-control cable enters the crankcase.   Slacken the lock-nut and screw home the cable adjusting-screw until some slackness of the cable is present.   Next slacken the lock-nut on the clutch push-rod adjusting screw which projects from the crankcase off-side cover in line with the gearbox mainshaft and just in front of the kick-starter spindle.

Turn the slotted adjuster screw *clockwise* until it begins to tighten and then turn it *one complete turn*.   This will ensure that the internal clutch-actuating lever is in its optimum position.   Afterwards re-tighten the lock-nut securely. Finally screw out the cable adjusting-screw until there is only about $\frac{1}{16}$ in. free movement of the clutch cable when operating the handlebar lever.   Tighten its lock-nut and push home the plastic sleeve.

Removing the Clutch Plates.   Remove the crankcase near-side cover (*see* page 32) and lock the rear wheel with top gear engaged.   Now, referring to Fig. 46, remove the three (six on early type "Crusader Sports"

GENERAL MAINTENANCE

models) hexagon-headed screws (*1*), the clutch spring retaining-plate (*2*), distance washers (where provided), and the front plate (*5*). Then on earlier 250 c.c. models remove the plates (*7*)–(*10*). On later 250 c.c. models it is necessary before removing these four plates to remove in this order: a friction-insert plate, and a plain plate.

If it is desired for some reason to remove the clutch sprocket, shown at (*4*) in Fig. 47, remove the slipper-type chain tensioner shown at (*7*) in

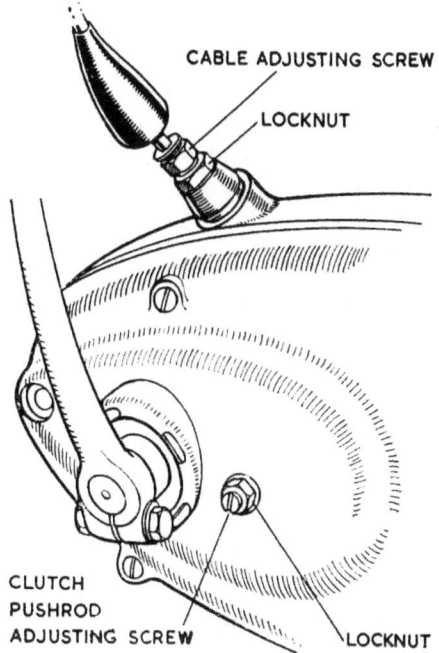

FIG. 45. SHOWING THE TWO CLUTCH ADJUSTMENTS
(*The Enfield Cycle Co. Ltd.*)

Fig. 32, slip the endless chain off the clutch sprocket, and withdraw the sprocket after removing its large circlip shown at (*5*) in Fig. 47.

Replacing the Clutch Plates. If the clutch sprocket has been removed, replace it on the clutch centre and secure with the large circlip (*see* Fig. 47). Be sure that the circlip beds right down in its groove. Position the primary chain on the sprocket teeth.

Referring to Fig. 46, assemble the plain steel and the friction-insert plates in the reverse order of removal. Be sure to replace all *dished* plates as shown at (*10*) in Fig. 46, with their *serrated centres facing outwards*. After replacing the clutch plates fit the clutch plate retaining-washer (*6*),

94 THE SECOND BOOK OF THE ROYAL ENFIELD

the distance washers (where provided), the front plate (*5*), the distance tubes (*4*), and the three or six springs (six on early "Crusader Sports" models). Then fit the clutch spring retaining-plate (*2*), followed by the three or six hexagon-headed screws (*1*). Finally replace the slipper-type primary chain tensioner shown at (*7*) in Fig. 32, adjust the tension of the

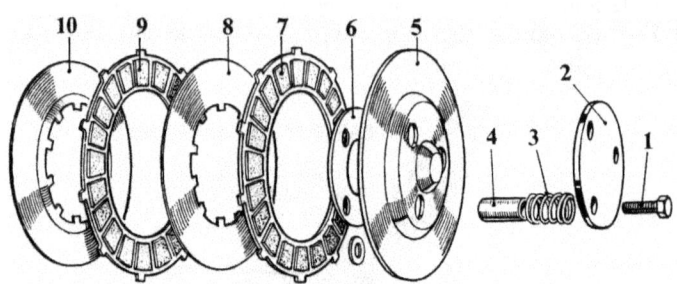

FIG. 46. THE CORRECT CLUTCH-PLATE ASSEMBLY ORDER FOR ALL EARLIER 250 C.C. MODELS

On all later 250, 350 c.c. models the assembly order is similar, but three friction-insert plates are provided for later 250 c.c. models and four for all 350 c.c. models. On all 1965 and later models the clutch sprocket has its friction inserts bonded on instead of riveted. All 350 c.c. machines have six clutch springs

1. Screw for compressing clutch spring
2. Spring retaining-plate
3. Clutch spring (three)
4. Distance tube (three)
5. Front plate (flat)
6. Clutch plate retaining-washer
7. Friction-insert plate
8. Plain intermediate plate
9. Friction-insert plate
10. Intermediate plate (dished)

(*The Enfield Cycle Co. Ltd.*)

primary chain (*see* page 66), and replace the crankcase near-side cover (*see* page 33).

To Remove and Replace the Clutch Centre. Removal of the clutch centre is not often necessary. Should it be necessary to remove it for any reason, first remove the clutch plates and clutch sprocket as previously described. Next, referring to Fig. 47, turn back the tab on the tab-washer (*2*) and remove the nut (*3*). Then with the Royal Enfield extractor (Part No. E.5414) withdraw the clutch centre from the taper on the gearbox mainshaft. Be most careful not to lose the small key.

When replacing the clutch centre on the gearbox mainshaft taper do not forget to fit the small key. Tighten the nut securely after replacing the tab-washer and bend over a tab. Renew the washer if not sound. Then replace the clutch sprocket and the clutch plates as previously described.

TRANSMISSION CHAINS

The Primary Chain. As the primary chain is completely enclosed by the crankcase near-side cover (*see* Fig. 44) it is automatically lubricated so long as the engine oil tank is regularly topped-up (*see* page 30). Every 2,000 on any other model with a pressed-steel chaincase (an optional extra) fitted, slacken the two screws (2) which secure the chaincase to the swinging arm. Then rotate the two cam-plate adjusters (3) clockwise or anti-clockwise, as required, to obtain correct chain tension.

When making an adjustment, endeavour to rotate the two cam-plates so that both have the same notch positions, but note that this does not guarantee that the front and rear wheels *are* in true alignment. Therefore after re-tightening both wheel-spindle nuts, and the two screws (2) where a chaincase is fitted, check the wheel alignment as described on page 106. An adjustment of the rear brake (*see* page 103) will also be necessary.

Secondary Chain Stretch. It is desirable to renew at once a secondary chain when its stretch exceeds $\frac{1}{4}$ in. per foot. To check for stretch, close up a foot length of the chain, measure the exact length, pull the links apart,

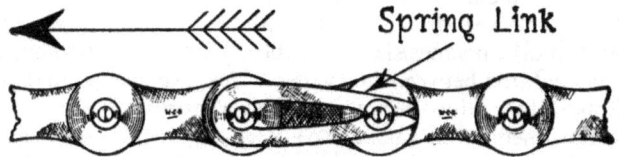

Fig. 50. ALWAYS FIT THE SPRING LINK LIKE THIS WHEN CONNECTING A SECONDARY CHAIN
To facilitate connecting the chain, join its two ends when positioned close together on the clutch sprocket

and again measure the chain length. The difference between the two lengths is, of course, the length of chain stretch.

Removing and Fitting Secondary Chain. Where the secondary chain is protected only by a chain guard, its removal for cleaning and greasing (*see* page 35), and its subsequent replacement over the sprockets, should present no difficulty. If the chain is completely protected by a chaincase (as on the "Crusader 250") regular oiling of the chain can be effected by removing the inspection plug shown at (1) in Fig. 49 and chain removal is not necessary until the chain requires renewal after a very big mileage. This should be done in the following manner.

Referring to Fig. 49, place the machine on its centre stand and withdraw the rear section (6) of the chaincase after removing the three securing screws (5) which secure it to the brake cover-plate. Now disconnect the secondary chain by removing its connecting link and join up the new chain (after greasing it) to the old one. Pull the new chain into the chaincase by pulling out the old chain. Then disconnect and remove the old chain and connect the ends of the new one. When fitting a secondary chain always make sure that the spring link is replaced as shown in Fig. 50.

This is extremely important because if the chain should come adrift when riding fast, a serious disaster can result. After fitting a new chain always check its chain tension (*see* page 96).

THE CUSH-DRIVE

How It Smooths Out Transmission. Royal Enfield motor-cycles are renowned for their transmission smoothness, due mainly to the incorporation of a patented cush-drive for the rear hub. This cush-drive effectively smooths out engine impulses at all speeds, prevents any tendency for transmission snatch to occur, and considerably reduces wear of the secondary chain and rear tyre.

The back of the brake drum (*see* Fig. 51) has three radial vanes, and three similar vanes are provided on the inside of the hub of a non-detachable type rear wheel or on the cush-drive shell which is secured to the hub of a quickly-detachable type rear wheel. When the brake drum is properly positioned on the cush-drive shell or on the rear hub there are therefore six vanes, those attached to the brake drum side being driving vanes, and those attached to the cush-drive shell, or hub, being driven vanes. Between the driving and driven vanes six solid rubber blocks (*4*) are fitted, each rubber block being fitted between two vanes. The expansion and contraction of the rubber blocks thus smooths out the transmission.

No adjustment of the cush-drive is necessary, but it is advisable whenever free movement of the rear wheel (with top gear engaged) becomes excessive (about 1 in. movement measured at the tyre tread) to remove the rear wheel, dismantle the cush-drive, and inspect the six rubber blocks (*4*) and the lock-ring (*2*). Renew them if appreciably worn. Their renewal is seldom necessary until at least 10,000 miles have been covered.

To Dismantle the Cush-drive. After removing the rear mudguard and dualseat unit (*see* page 108) remove the non-detachable or quickly-detachable type rear wheel (*see* pages 108, 111). Note that a quickly-detachable type rear wheel (fitted to all models except the "250 Clipper") must be removed *complete*, and the main portion of the wheel afterwards detached as follows. Unscrew and remove the off-side (loose) section of the wheel spindle with its distance collar, cam-plate, and washer attached. Then withdraw the wheel and hub assembly (which has six driving pins) from the near-side assembly comprising the near-side (fixed) section of the spindle; the brake drum with its integral sprocket; the brake cover-plate with its shoe assembly; and the cush-drive shell with its six rubber blocks. Then from a non-detachable or quickly-detachable type rear wheel, dismantle the cush-drive assembly as described below.

Remove the near-side spindle nut, washer, cam-plate, and distance collar (*see* Fig. 55). Now lift off the brake cover-plate, complete with brake-shoe assembly. On a non-detachable type wheel remove the three Simmonds nuts from the near-side hub flange. On a quickly-detachable wheel, referring to Fig. 51, unscrew the three nuts (*7*) located at the back of

GENERAL MAINTENANCE 99

the cush-drive shell (5) after bending back the tabs of the three tab-washers (6). Then drive out from the hub flange or the cush-drive shell into the brake drum (3) the three studs brazed to the large lock-ring (2). To avoid damaging the lock-ring or studs apply a hammer evenly to all three studs, tapping them out in rotation. Finally remove the brake drum and integral

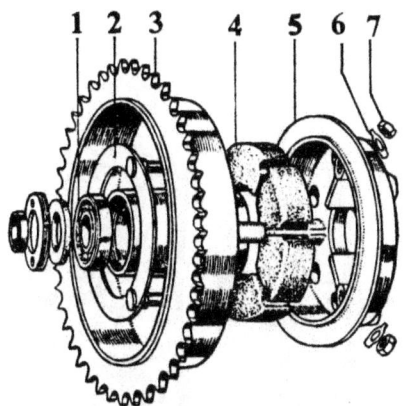

FIG. 51. THE BRAKE DRUM AND CUSH-DRIVE ASSEMBLY REMOVED FROM A QUICKLY-DETACHABLE REAR WHEEL

On a non-detachable type wheel (as fitted to the "250 Clipper") the brake drum and lock-ring (2) are secured direct to the hub flange of the rear wheel

1. Ball bearing pressed into the hub of 3
2. Lock-ring with three brazed studs for securing 3 to cush-drive shell
3. Brake drum with integral sprocket
4. Solid-rubber blocks (six)
5. Cush-drive shell
6. Tab-washer for 7
7. Nut (three) for securing 2, 3 to cush-drive shell 5

(*The Enfield Cycle Co. Ltd.*)

sprocket from the wheel hub or cush-drive shell. Lift out the six rubber blocks (4) for inspection and renewal if necessary.

Assembling the Cush-drive. When replacing or renewing the six rubber blocks, position them in the hub housing or the detachable cush-drive shell so that they lean against each other as shown in Fig. 52. This will facilitate the entry of the brake-drum vanes between them. To further facilitate entry, smear all the rubber blocks with soapsuds.

Prior to securing the brake drum to the hub of a non-detachable type wheel or to the cush-drive shell of a quickly-detachable type, grease the inside of the brake-drum bore where it fits over the hub barrel. Also grease the inner face of the lock-ring. Tap home firmly the three studs brazed to the lock-ring and before fitting the nuts on a quickly-detachable wheel replace the three tab-washers. Tighten down the nuts very securely. Locking of the cush-drive is impossible because the studs have shoulders. Bend over the tabs of the tab-washers where fitted.

Replace the brake cover-plate, complete with shoe assembly, and fit on the spindle the distance collar, cam-plate, and washer and nut. Tighten the nut lightly. A non-detachable type wheel can now be replaced in the motor-cycle fork ends (*see* page 109). Where a quickly-detachable type rear wheel is concerned, the wheel and hub assembly must first be fitted to the brake drum, brake cover-plate, and cush-drive assembly. The off-side (loose) section of the wheel spindle should be partly screwed home after

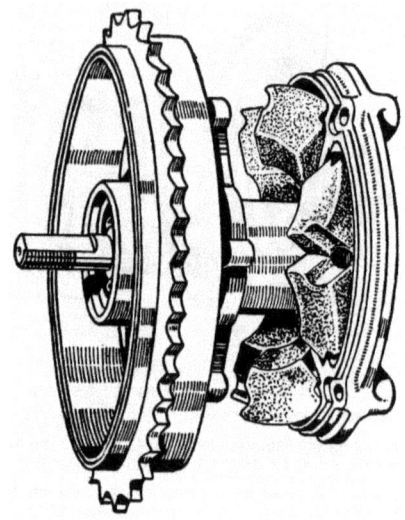

FIG. 52. HOW THE SIX RUBBER BLOCKS SHOULD BE POSITIONED IN THE CUSH-DRIVE SHELL TO PROVIDE A LEAD FOR THE BRAKE-DRUM VANES

The cush-drive shell is shown removed from a quickly-detachable rear wheel after the complete wheel has been removed from the motor-cycle rear-fork ends
(*The Enfield Cycle Co. Ltd.*)

replacing the distance collar, cam-plate, and washer. The wheel can then be fitted to the motor-cycle (*see* page 111).

CARE OF TYRES

To Obtain Good Tyre Mileage. Modern tyres of reputable make, such as the ribbed and studded wired-on Dunlop types fitted to all new Royal Enfield motor-cycles, are very robust and scientifically designed for a very big mileage if properly treated. To obtain the maximum trouble-free mileage from your tyres you should avoid the following: (*a*) riding with incorrect tyre pressures; (*b*) riding with the front and rear wheels out of true alignment; (*c*) sudden braking; (*d*) fierce acceleration; (*e*) fast cornering at an angle; (*f*) careless use of the clutch when gear changing; (*g*) allowing oil or paraffin to remain on the tyres; (*h*) neglecting to remove small stones or flints embedded in the tyre treads. Punctures can often be

GENERAL MAINTENANCE

avoided by digging out stones or flints with a small pocket-knife. The cuts can then be filled with a proprietary tyre-stopping compound if available.

Always Keep Tyre Pressures Correct. It is advisable to check the tyre pressures *weekly*, and always before starting off on a long run. Suitable tyre-pressure gauges (obtainable from most accessory firms) are the Dunlop pencil type No. 6, the Romac, the Schrader No. 7750, and the Holdtite. Correctly inflated tyres provide comfortable riding, reduce any tendency for skidding, and last longer than those which are not correctly inflated.

Under-inflation tends to cause the tyres to creep, cracking of the tyre covers due to internal casing strains, and instability of steering. Over-inflation strains the covers, causes vibration, and a tendency for a concussion burst to occur. All Royal Enfields dealt with in this handbook have 3·25—17 in. tyres, and the correct tyre pressures for 250 and 350 c.c. models are—

Front Tyre: 18 lb per sq in.
Rear Tyre (Solo): 22 lb per sq in.
Rear Tyre (with Pillion Rider): 30 lb per sq in.

When riding solo the pressure for the rear tyre should be increased slightly if the rider is above average weight or carries heavy equipment. After pumping up the tyres to the correct pressures never forget to replace the two valve dust-caps. This is important.

Tyre Removal. Tyre removal is seldom necessary these days except when it is required to renew an inner tube and/or tyre cover. Road surfaces and tyres are both good and punctures are rare. Should a puncture occur and its exact position is known, the complete removal of an inner tube is often unnecessary. Where the location of a puncture is not known it is, of course, necessary to remove the complete inner tube, preceded by the removal of one side of the cover. To remove one side of the cover, or to remove the cover where renewal is required, the front or rear wheel should be removed (*see* pages 106–11). If a non-detachable type rear wheel is fitted, as on the "250 Clipper," it is, however, possible to remove the complete inner tube without disturbing the rear wheel (*see* page 102).

The two small tyre-levers provided in the Royal Enfield tool-kit are quite sufficient for tyre removal and replacement. The use of long levers and/or excessive force is undesirable as this imposes an undue strain on the tyre casing. To remove an inner tube and the tyre cover from the rim if necessary, proceed as follows.

First with the key formed in the dust-cap unscrew the inside of the valve and deflate the tyre. Also free the valve from the wheel rim by removing its knurled lock-nut. Next press both walls of the tyre cover, at a point opposite to the valve, down into the well in the centre of the wheel rim, and work the walls down into the well as far as possible in both directions.

Then insert the two small tyre-levers, one on each side of the valve, and about 6 in. apart, and proceed to lever off the side of the cover. No undue force should be needed provided that the edges of the cover opposite the valve are right down in the well. When the whole of one side has been levered off the wheel rim, withdraw the inner tube. Remove the cover completely if its condition calls for renewal. A tyre with a worn-off tread besides being likely to result in punctures, is most dangerous.

Replacing a Tyre. Dust the inner tube with some French chalk, slightly inflate it, and replace it inside the cover, assuming that the cover has not been completely removed or that one side of a new cover has been positioned on the rim. Lever the side of the cover into position, starting *opposite to the valve* and finishing close to it, with the edge of the cover at the opposite side of the wheel pressed down into the wheel rim. Inflate the tyre to a moderate extent and make sure that the wired edges of the cover are in their proper places and not down in the well. A fine line moulded on the wall of the tyre near its rim should be about $\frac{1}{4}$ in. from the wheel rim all the way round if the cover is correctly fitted. Afterwards pump up the tyre to the correct pressure (*see* page 101), replace the knurled lock-nut on the valve stem, and fit the dust-cap to the valve.

Note Concerning New Tyres. To assist smooth riding, precise steering, and tread life, Dunlop motor-cycle tyres are balanced to prescribed limits. Note that if a new tyre has a white mark this indicates a balance point. If it has, the tyre should be fitted so that the balance point is near the valve of the inner tube.

Quick Removal of an Inner Tube. Where a non-detachable type rear wheel is fitted (as on the "250 Clipper") instead of a quickly-detachable type, it is possible to remove the inner tube for puncture repair or renewal without removing the wheel from the frame. To do this, first deflate the tyre and with two tyre-levers remove the off-side of the tyre from the wheel rim. Next, referring to Fig. 53, unscrew and remove the centre bolt (*1*). Spring the rear fork-ends apart slightly to free the slip-collar (*2*) from the spigot locating it, and slide the collar out of the fork end. Then disconnect the speedometer driving-cable from the speedometer gearbox, remove the inner tube from the tyre cover, and carefully withdraw the tube through the space provided between the speedometer gearbox and the inside of the frame fork end.

BRAKE MAINTENANCE

To Ensure Powerful Braking. Always apply the front and rear brakes together, otherwise unnecessary wear of the linings on the rear brake-shoes occurs. Under present traffic conditions powerful braking is quite often necessary. Therefore always keep the front and rear brakes adjusted so that the brake-shoe linings are in close contact with the brake drums but do not bind when the brakes are released. After adjusting each brake, test for free rotation of the wheel by spinning it by hand with the wheel clear of the ground.

Front Brake Adjustment. To adjust the front brake to take up shoe-lining wear and cable stretch, turn the knurled self-locking adjuster nut

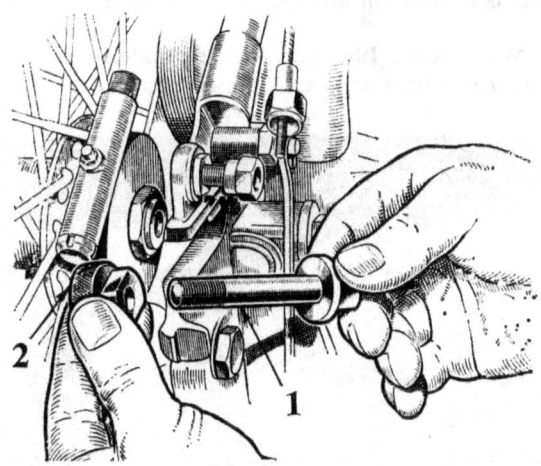

FIG. 53. WHERE A NON-DETACHABLE TYPE REAR WHEEL IS PROVIDED AN INNER TUBE CAN QUICKLY BE REMOVED

The only dismantling necessary is to remove the centre bolt *1* and the slip-collar *2*. All 1958–66 models except the "250 Clipper" have a quickly-detachable rear wheel necessitating the removal of the main part of the wheel or, if the brake shoes or cush-drive require attention, the complete wheel assembly

(*The Enfield Cycle Co. Ltd.*)

mounted on the brake anchor-plate or low down on the near-side of the telescopic forks as required.

Rear Brake Adjustment. Before adjusting the rear brake, referring to Fig. 54, make sure that the brake pedal is set in the best position for convenient operation. If necessary, adjust by means of the pedal-stop provided. To raise or lower the pedal position, loosen the lock-nut (*3*) and turn the adjustable pedal-stop screw (*2*) clockwise or anti-clockwise as required.

With the brake-pedal position set suitably, adjust the rear brake to take up shoe-lining wear by turning the wing nut (shown at (*4*) in Fig. 49) on the threaded end of the brake rod as required.

If Grease Gets On the Linings. It is most unlikely for grease to find its way on to the brake linings, provided that the correct type of grease (*see* page 36) is used when repacking the hub bearings about every 10,000 miles. Should the brake linings inside a brake drum lose their efficiency through this cause, the only remedy is to remove the brake shoes concerned and scrape all grease off the linings. When doing this care should be taken not to rough them up. Clean the linings with some petrol. When reassembly is completed, ride with the brake partly on and in second gear for about half a mile so as to burn off any grease which remains.

Renewing Worn Brake Linings. The internal-expanding brakes have drums of cast iron which are free from any tendency for scoring. The

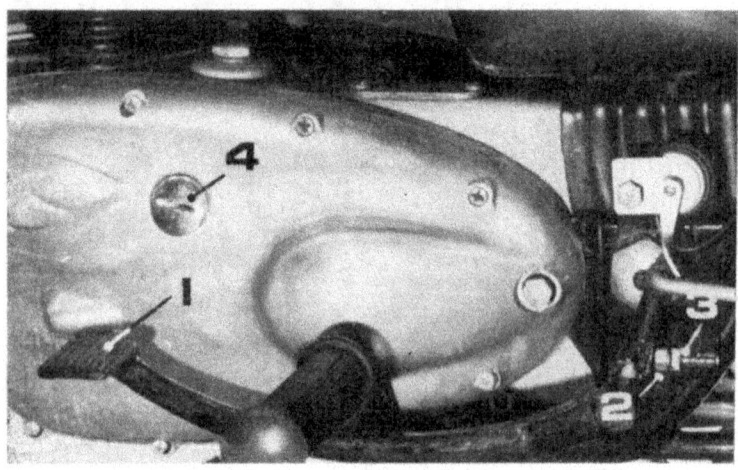

Fig. 54. Showing Adjustment for Rear-brake Pedal Position, and Inspection Cap for Checking Primary Chain Tension
 1. Rear-brake pedal
 2. Adjustable pedal-stop screw
 3. Lock-nut for 2
 4. Inspection cap for checking primary chain tension

brake shoes are lined with a special moulded material (Ferodo AM2) which wears very slowly if you do not indulge in persistent fierce braking. After a prolonged mileage, however, it is inevitable that braking efficiency is lost through wear of the linings.

Where brake lining renewal is necessary, remove the wheel or wheels concerned (*see* pages 106–11) and remove the brake shoes as described later. Either exchange your brake shoes with service-replacement shoes (obtainable from a Royal Enfield dealer) or else obtain linings which are supplied in pairs ready drilled and complete with cheese-headed rivets. If you decide to rivet new linings on to your own shoes, note that you must secure the two *centre* rivets for each shoe first, to ensure that the lining lies flat against the brake shoe. Note that earlier type "Crusader 250" models have their brake linings bonded on to the shoes. Where excessive lining wear occurs, these shoes must be returned to the makers for servicing.

To Remove Brake Shoes (Front Wheel). Remove the front wheel (*see* page 106). Then while applying pressure on the operating lever to expand the shoes, unscrew the brake cover-plate nut and withdraw the cover-plate assembly from the brake drum, complete with operating lever, cam, pivot-pin (non-detachable), brake shoes, and return springs. Detach the return springs and remove both brake shoes.

To Remove Brake Shoes (Rear Wheel). Remove the non-detachable or quickly-detachable type rear wheel. If the wheel is of the latter type, the

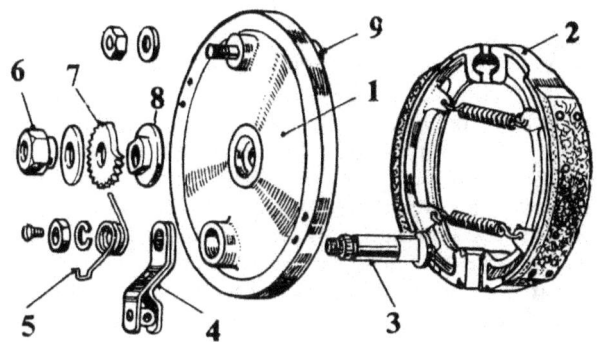

FIG. 55. THE REAR BRAKE COVER-PLATE, BRAKE-SHOE ASSEMBLY, ETC.

1. Cover plate
2. Shoe assembly
3. Operating cam
4. Operating lever
5. Return spring for 4
6. Hub-spindle nut (near-side)
7. Cam-plate adjuster for chain tension
8. Distance collar
9. Shoe pivot-pin (not detachable)

(*The Enfield Cycle Co. Ltd.*)

complete wheel must, of course, be removed. Rear wheel removal is dealt with on pages 109–11. Next remove the spindle nut, the washer, the cam-plate adjuster for the chain, and the distance collar. Then withdraw the cover-plate assembly (*see* Fig. 55) from the hub spindle, complete with operating lever, cam, pivot-pin (non-detachable), brake shoes, and return springs. Remove both brake shoes after detaching the return springs. Replacing the shoes should present no difficulty.

Assembling the Brake Shoes. This should present no difficulty. Smear a little grease on the face of the operating cam and also on the pivot-pin before replacing the brake cover-plate.

Altering Brake Operating-lever Position. If the brake linings are considerably worn but enough Ferodo material is left to be reasonably efficient, it may be found that the operating lever on the outside of the brake cover-plate assumes an angle which causes inefficient braking when the brake is hard on. The remedy in this case is, referring to Fig. 55, to remove the operating lever (*4*) from the splines on the operating cam (*3*) and replace it on a different spline to suit the extent of lining wear. The limit of lining wear is reached when the operating cam turns through 90 degrees.

FRONT AND REAR WHEELS

The Wheel Bearings. The hubs of both wheels have deep-groove single-row journal ball bearings. These require no adjustment at all, and they need lubricating only about every 10,000 miles (*see* page 36).

Wheel Alignment. To ensure good steering and to prevent a tendency for skidding and uneven wear of the tyre treads, the front and rear wheels must be kept truly aligned. Unless special care is taken when moving the cam-plate adjusters (*see* Fig. 49), it is necessary to check wheel alignment after adjusting the tension of the secondary chain (*see* page 96) and also after removing and replacing the rear wheel.

Note that the wheels are not necessarily correctly aligned when the same notch position is used for both cam-plate adjusters. However, once the positions of the adjusters giving true alignment have been obtained, the cam-plates can be marked. True alignment can then always be maintained, provided that both cam-plate adjusters are subsequently moved the same number of notches from the marks.

To check the wheel alignment where the cam-plate adjusters have not been marked, or when symptoms of bad alignment are present, place a straight-edge or a board alongside the two wheels. It should touch the tyres (which are of the same size) at four points when the handlebars are moved to the normal riding position, with the machine on its centre stand. An alternative method of checking wheel alignment is to use a taut piece of string secured to an anchorage point (*see* Fig. 56).

To Remove Front Wheel. First place your motor-cycle on its centre stand with about 2 in. of packing inserted under each side of the stand to raise the front wheel clear of the ground when the rear wheel is tilted back on to it. To keep the rear wheel on the ground it is advisable to put a weight on the dualseat.

Disconnect the front-brake cable by slackening the knurled self-locking cable-adjuster nut and freeing the cable from the operating-cam lever on the brake cover-plate. On the 1962-3 "Crusader Super 5" with leading-link type front forks also disconnect the brake anchor-arm by removing the securing nut and pushing out the pin which secures the anchor arm to the near-side fork-leg bracket. Remove the four nuts (shown at (*3*) in Fig. 57)

FIG. 56. CHECKING WHEEL ALIGNMENT WITH A TAUT PIECE OF STRING

If wheel alignment is correct, the string (*A*) should contact the front and rear tyres at the four points indicated by white dots. An alternative check is to place a straight-edge or board alongside the wheels. When the alignment is correct, mark the two cam-plate adjusters (*see* text) for the rear wheel. The motor-cycle illustrated above is the latest version of the popular 1959–66 250 c.c. "Crusader Sports" model (*see* Preface)

(*The Enfield Cycle Co. Ltd.*)

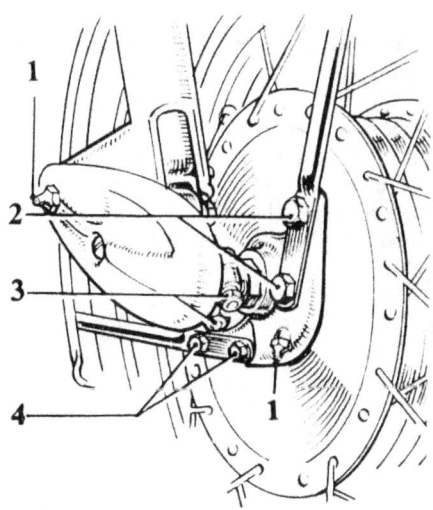

FIG. 57. ON THE LATER "CRUSADER SUPER 5" AND THE 1965 "OLYMPIC" THE FRONT MUDGUARD IS ATTACHED TO THE WHEEL HUB ASSEMBLY, AND BOTH SHOULD BE REMOVED TOGETHER

1. Grease nipples (four)
2. Screws securing mudguard front stay
3. Nuts securing wheel spindle retaining-caps to forks
4. Screws securing mudguard rear stay

which secure the wheel spindle retaining-caps to the bottom ends of the telescopic-fork legs and withdraw the front wheel, complete with the front mudguard in the case of the later "Crusader Super 5." On this machine to remove the front mudguard after wheel removal, in order to remove the tyre or front brake cover-plate, remove the eight screws, shown at (*2*), (*4*) in Fig. 57, which secure the four mudguard chain-stays to the wheel hub.

Replacing the Front Wheel. On a later "Crusader Super 5" first replace the front mudguard on the wheel hub and secure it by firmly tightening the eight chain-stay attachment screws. Then position the wheel spindle in the front-fork ends and fit the two retaining caps, washers, and cap-securing nuts. Tighten all four nuts evenly and firmly. Connect up the front-brake anchor arm to the fork bracket by pushing home the pin and tightening its securing nut. Finally reconnect the front-brake cable to the operating-cam lever on the near-side of the hub and adjust the front brake (*see* page 103).

Removing and Replacing the Rear-mudguard Unit. On all models the rear mudguard, the mudguard carrier, and the dualseat comprise a single unit which can quickly be removed and replaced when it is necessary to remove and replace a non-detachable type rear wheel or a quickly-detachable type.

To remove the rear mudguard unit, first loosen the two nuts securing the top ends of the Girling rear-suspension units to the two frame brackets and push back the two bolts about $\frac{1}{8}$ in. to free their heads from the recesses on the inside of the mudguard-unit carrier brackets. Disconnect the lead to the stop-tail lamp. Now, standing at the rear of the motor-cycle, grasp its lifting handles (where fitted) and pull the mudguard unit *upwards* until the attachment brackets clear the respective nuts and bolt heads. Then pull the unit *backwards* until the clip at the front of the mudguard carrier disengages the back-stay bridge-tube of the frame and allows the unit to be withdrawn.

When replacing the rear-mudguard unit first engage the clip at the front of the mudguard carrier with the back-stay bridge-tube of the frame and lower the unit into position. When tightening the nuts on the bolts securing the Girling rear-suspension units, make quite sure that the bolt heads are right home in the recesses on the insides of the mudguard carrier attachment-brackets.

To Remove Rear Wheel (Non-detachable Type). On a "250 Clipper," which is not provided with a quickly-detachable type rear wheel, first remove the rear mudguard unit as previously described, and pull the motor-cycle on to its centre stand, preferably with some packing inserted beneath the legs of the stand to raise the rear wheel clear of the ground. Then use the following dismantling procedure to remove the rear wheel.

Disconnect the secondary chain at its spring link and remove the chain from the rear-wheel sprocket. Do not remove it from the gearbox-countershaft sprocket. Unscrew and remove completely the wing nut from the rear brake rod and depress the brake pedal to disengage the rod from the trunnion in the brake operating-lever. Disconnect the brake cover-plate from the rear fork lug, removing the anchor nut and the washer behind it. Unscrew the hexagon-nut which connects the speedometer driving cable to the speedometer gearbox, and withdraw the cable. Now loosen the spindle nut on the near-side and the centre bolt (*see* Fig. 58) on the off-side and slide the rear wheel out of the fork ends after marking

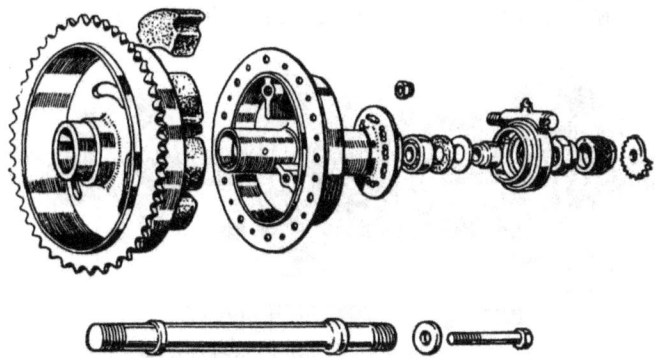

Fig. 58. Exploded View of Hub of Non-detachable Type Rear Wheel
The hub spindle and the centre bolt are shown below the hub assembly. Not shown are the lock-ring (*see* Fig. 51) securing the brake drum to the hub flange, the brake-shoe assembly, and its cover plate (*see* Fig. 55)
(*The Enfield Cycle Co. Ltd.*)

the cam-plate adjusters (*see* page 106) to ensure correct wheel alignment after assembly. When sliding the wheel out, tilt it so as to disengage the end of the brake-shoe pivot-pin from the slot in the fork end.

Replacing Rear Wheel (Non-detachable Type). Replace the wheel in the reverse order of removal. The following points should be noted: see that the dogs on the speedometer-drive gearbox engage with the slots in the end of the hub barrel; be sure that the speedometer-drive gearbox is correctly positioned so as to avoid any sudden bend in the driving cable; when connecting the secondary chain, see that the open end of the spring link faces away from the direction of chain travel; replace the cam-plate adjusters for chain tension in their original positions (*see* page 106) to ensure correct wheel alignment, or subsequently check the alignment. After assembly is completed, check the rear brake adjustment (*see* page 102).

To Remove Main Portion of Rear Wheel (Quickly-detachable Type). All Royal Enfield models except the "250 Clipper" have a quickly-detachable type rear wheel. With this type it is possible for tyre repairs to remove the main portion of the rear wheel without disturbing the rear mudguard, the secondary chain, the brake adjustment, the brake cover-plate with its shoe assembly, the brake drum, or the cush-drive assembly.

Place your motor-cycle on its centre stand, unscrew the off-side spindle nut, and remove the loose section of the wheel spindle (*see* Fig. 59), together with the washer and cam-plate adjuster for secondary chain tension. Mark the adjuster to ensure that it is subsequently replaced in the same position, assuming that chain tension (*see* page 96) and wheel alignment (*see* page 105) were previously correct. Next withdraw the distance collar from the off-side fork end and remove the speedometer-drive gearbox with

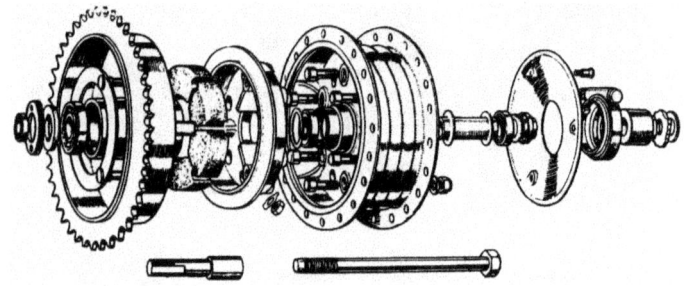

FIG. 59. EXPLODED VIEW OF HUB OF QUICKLY-DETACHABLE TYPE REAR WHEEL

The fixed and loose portions of the hub spindle are shown below the cush-drive assembly and the hub assembly respectively. Not shown are the brake-shoe assembly and its cover plate (*see* Fig. 55)

(*The Enfield Cycle Co. Ltd.*)

its driving cable attached. Also remove the spacing collar and the adjacent felt washer unless they are a tight fit in the hub. In this case do not disturb them.

Pull the main portion of the rear wheel over to the off-side of the machine so as to disengage the six hub driving-pins from the shell of the cush-drive assembly. Finally, while standing on the near-side of the motor-cycle, adjacent to the rear mudguard, tilt the machine over to the left until the quickly-detachable wheel can be rolled out between the rear mudguard and the off-side fork end.

Replacing Main Portion of Rear Wheel (Quickly-detachable Type). To replace the main portion of the wheel use the removal procedure just described in reverse. Observe the following: when replacing the speedometer-drive gearbox make sure that the driving dogs inside it engage the slots in the end of the wheel-hub barrel; to prevent the cush-drive shell rotating while turning the rear wheel to engage its six driving pins with the shell, engage a gear, or alternatively depress the rear brake pedal; prior to tightening the centre spindle, position the speedometer-drive gearbox so that its driving cable has no sharp bend.

GENERAL MAINTENANCE

To Remove Complete Rear Wheel (Quickly-detachable Type). If it is desired to remove the brake cover-plate in order to inspect or renew the brake-shoe linings (*see* page 104) or to dismantle the cush-drive (*see* page 98) in order to inspect and if necessary renew the lock-ring and six rubber blocks, it is obviously necessary to remove the complete rear wheel. Do this as described below.

Jack up your motor-cycle on its centre stand and first remove the rear mudguard unit (*see* page 108). If the secondary chain is completely enclosed in a chaincase, remove the five small screws securing the rear and front portions of it to the rear brake cover-plate (*see* Fig. 49). Withdraw the rear portion of the chaincase. Disconnect the secondary chain at its spring link and loop the upper end of the chain over the tag provided at the top of the fixed portion of the chaincase. Pull on the other end of the secondary chain and allow it to hang from the lower tunnel of the chaincase. This will prevent the chain disappearing inside the chaincase, a most annoying occurrence!

Remove the wing nut for adjusting the rear brake and depress the brake pedal so as to disengage the brake operating-rod from the trunnion in the brake operating-lever. Remove the anchor nut, and the washer behind it, from the brake cover-plate. Unscrew the loose section of the spindle two or three turns (*see* Fig. 59). Similarly unscrew the spindle nut. Mark both the cam-plate adjusters provided for maintaining correct chain tension (*see* page 96) and wheel alignment (*see* page 105) to ensure their correct replacement. Now disconnect the speedometer driving-cable and carefully slide the quickly-detachable rear wheel out of the fork ends. To disengage the end of the brake-shoe pivot on the brake cover-plate from the slot in the fork end, tilt the wheel as required while sliding it out.

Replacing Complete Rear Wheel (Quickly-detachable Type). Replace the wheel in the reverse order of removal. Do not overlook the following points. See that the driving dogs inside the speedometer-drive gearbox engage the slots in the end of the wheel-hub barrel. Also position the gearbox so that there is no acute bend in its driving cable. When replacing the secondary chain over the brake drum sprocket make sure that its spring link is fitted as shown in Fig. 50. Replace the two cam-plate adjusters for the secondary chain in their original positions if marked. If not marked, turn them the same number of notches and afterwards check the tension of the secondary chain (*see* page 96) and the wheel alignment (*see* page 96). Where an adjustment of the chain tension is required on a machine with the chain enclosed in a chaincase, the front section of the chaincase first needs re-positioning. Loosen the two screws (shown at (2) in Fig. 49) which secure it to the swinging arm *before* securing the chaincase to the rear brake cover-plate by means of the two small screws. After replacing the rear-brake rod and fitting its wing-nut adjuster, adjust the rear brake correctly (*see* page 103).

STEERING-HEAD ADJUSTMENT

The steering-head bearings comprise two deep-groove thrust races, each containing nineteen ¼ in. diameter balls. Excessive play or friction in the bearings rapidly causes damage and an adjustment is provided on all models. Wear of the thrust races gradually occurs and a check should occasionally be made to see if play exists. The steering-head adjustment is identical on all models except the 1962–3 250 c.c. "Crusader Super 5"

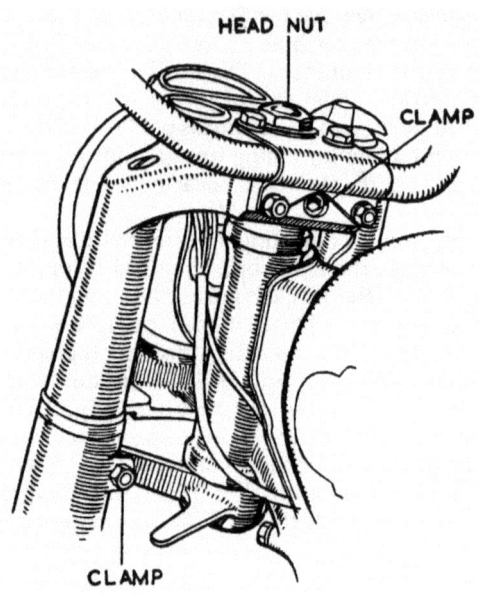

FIG. 60. STEERING-HEAD ADJUSTMENT ON ALL 1958–66 MODELS EXCEPT THE 1962–3 "CRUSADER SUPER 5" AND THE 1965 "OLYMPIC"
(*The Enfield Cycle Co. Ltd.*)

and the 1965 250 c.c. "Olympic." These machines have a special leading-link design of telescopic front forks with a different type of steering-head adjustment.

To Adjust (All 1958–66 Models Except the 1962–3 "Crusader Super 5" and the 1965 "Olympic"). Referring to Fig. 60, to adjust the steering-head ball races where play exists, first loosen the steering head clamp (a wedge bolt). Also loosen the two clamps (bolts) at the fork crown. Then tighten down as required the large hexagon nut on top of the steering stem. The steering-head adjustment is correct when, with the front wheel lifted clear of the ground, the steering is such that: (*a*) a light push on the handlebars in either direction causes the steering to swing over freely to

GENERAL MAINTENANCE 113

full lock; (b) no perceptible up-and-down play is felt. The special rubber rings above the upper main-tube covers allow for distance variation when the above adjustment is made. After making the required adjustment, securely tighten the three clamp-bolts.

To Adjust (1962–3 "Crusader Super 5" and 1965 "Olympic"). To make a steering-head adjustment first remove the weight from the front wheel by inserting a suitable box under the crankcase of the engine. Next slacken the head clamp-bolt located under the handlebars. Also remove the large central nut and thick washer from the top of the steering head. Then to take up bearing play, carefully tighten down the slotted sleeve until no perceptible up-and-down play is felt. It should be possible for the steering to swing over to full lock in either direction when the handlebars are given a slight push. After making the necessary adjustment tighten the head clamp-bolt and replace the thick washer and large central nut on top of the steering head.

FRONT AND REAR SUSPENSION

The telescopic front forks fitted to all 1958–66 models are of identical type except in the case of the 1962–3 250 c.c. "Crusader Super 5" and the 1965 250 c.c. "Olympic" which have leading-link type front forks of an entirely different design. On all models the rear suspension comprises two swinging arms used in conjunction with two Girling type rear-suspension units filled with hydraulic damping oil.

The Telescopic Front Forks. On all models except the 1962–3 "Crusader Super 5" and the 1965 "Olympic" very occasionally and *when necessary* top-up the front forks with hydraulic damping oil. The correct topping-up procedure and suitable damping oils to use are dealt with on page 35. On the "Crusader Super 5" and "Olympic" every 500 miles inject some grease through the grease nipples shown at (*1*) in Fig. 57. The telescopic front forks require no other maintenance other than to keep the hub-spindle securing nuts and external bolts tight, and the steering-head adjustment (*see* page 112) correct.

To Dismantle Front Forks (All Models Except "Crusader Super 5" and "Olympic"). Dismantling the front-fork legs is rarely necessary unless it is desired to renew the springs. The following is the procedure required. With the motor-cycle on its centre stand, remove the front wheel (*see* page 106). Also remove the mudguard, complete with its stays. Remove the plug screw from the top of each fork leg (*see* Fig. 61) and withdraw, from the lower end of the main tube, the sliding member of the fork leg, complete with spring and spring distance-tube. Tap the bolt protruding from the sliding member until it is free, remembering that as the bolt is freed oil escapes from the tube. Then unscrew the spring distance-tube from the spring and unscrew the spring from the sliding member of the fork leg.

A Useful Tip. Should it for some reason be necessary to remove the fork-leg main tube, loosen the corresponding clamp-bolt at the fork crown and with a special key applied to the internal hexagon from above the

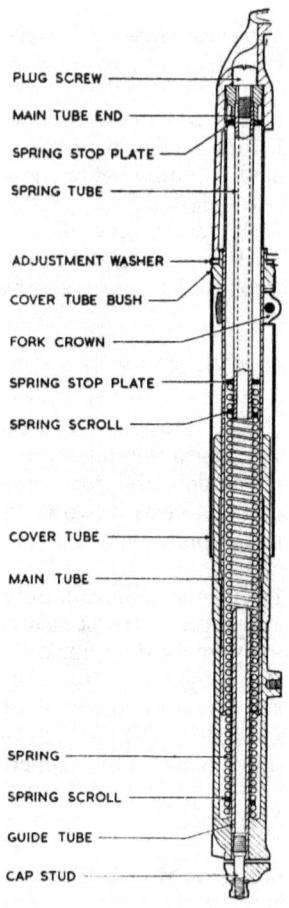

Fig. 61. Sectional View of Front-fork Leg (all 1958–66 Models Except the "Crusader Super 5" and "Olympic")
(*The Enfield Cycle Co. Ltd.*)

"casquette," unscrew the tube. Where a special key is not available, use the footrest-hanger rod which is of the right size and hexagonal. Insert the rod into the top of the fork tube and apply a spanner to the projecting length of rod. This useful tip can save a lot of bother.

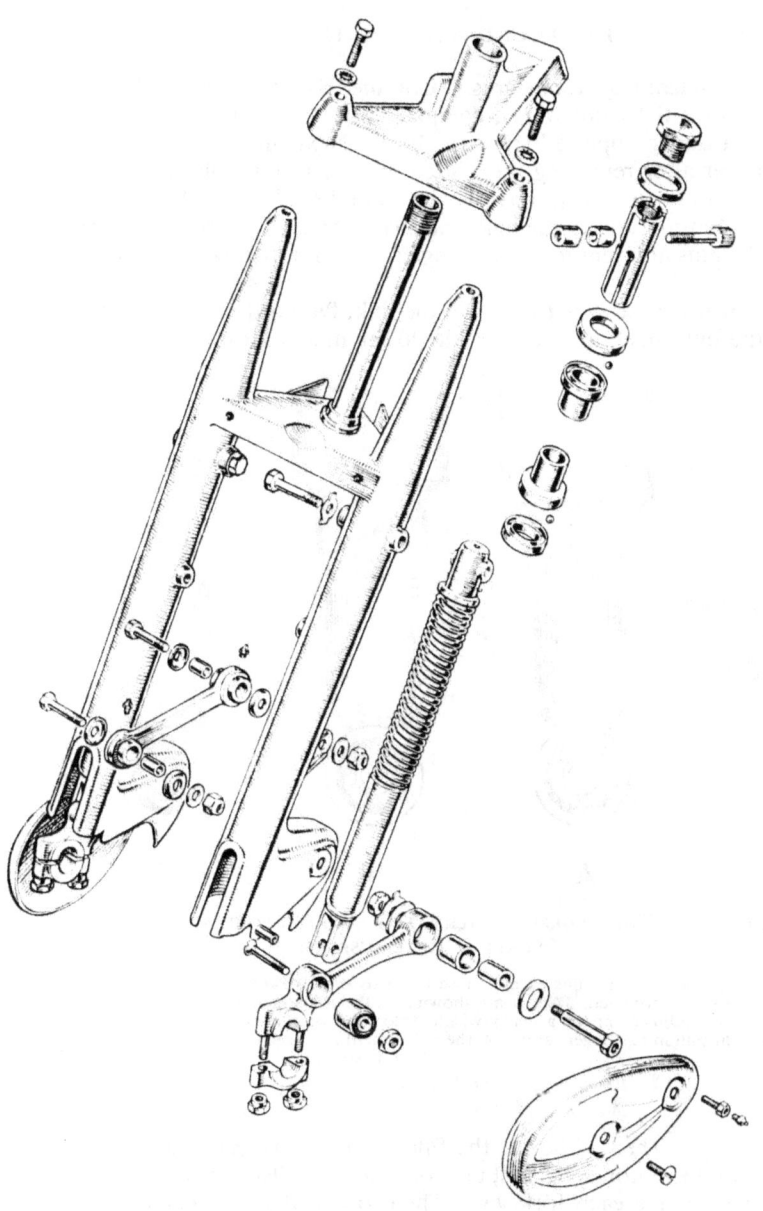

Fig. 62. Exploded View of Leading-link Type Front Forks and Steering Head ("Crusader Super 5" and "Olympic")
(*The Enfield Cycle Co. Ltd.*)

Dismantling Front Forks ("Crusader Super 5" and "Olympic"). First remove the front wheel, complete with front mudguard on a later type "Crusader Super 5" (*see* page 106). Next withdraw each moulded side-cover after removing the slotted screw and the bolt in the pivot-pin (*see* Fig. 62). Also withdraw the pin from the rubber bush which connects the suspension unit to the link, and swing the link downwards. Now remove the pins adjacent to the steering crown, and then withdraw the suspension unit.

If it is necessary to remove the link, flatten the tab-washer and remove the nut which also secures the lower mudguard-bracket to the inside of

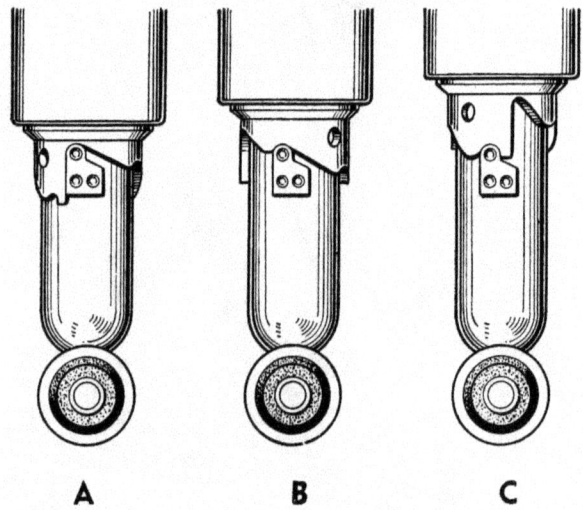

FIG. 63. THE THREE ALTERNATIVE SPRING-LOADING ADJUSTMENTS FOR GIRLING REAR-SUSPENSION UNITS

All rear-suspension units except those fitted to the 1958–65 "250 Clipper" have alternative adjustments provided. Above are shown at *A* the adjustment for a medium-weight solo rider; at *B* the adjustment for a heavy-weight solo rider or a medium-weight rider with medium-weight pillion passenger; and at *C* the adjustment for a heavy-weight rider with heavy-weight pillion passenger

(*B.S.A. Motor Cycles Ltd.*)

the leg. Then withdraw the fulcrum pin. To remove the fork leg unit from the motor-cycle, first take out the two Allen screws from the steering head to free each fork leg. Then loosen the steering-head clamp bolt, remove the large nut and tab-washer from the top of the steering head, and unscrew the slotted sleeve until it clears the steering stem.

The Swinging-arm Pivot. On some machines this requires greasing about every 500 miles (*see* page 37).

The Girling Rear-suspension Units. Except on the 1958–65 "250 Clipper" the bottom cup for the suspension spring of each unit can be adjusted with the "C" spanner in the tool-kit to one of three alternative positions (*see* Fig. 63) to suit rear loading. To ensure comfortable riding without any excessive up-and-down movement make the adjustment to suit your weight and that of your pillon rider if carried.

Girling rear-suspension units need no topping-up with damping oil. They are in fact sealed. Unless appreciable internal wear occurs there is no risk of oil leakage. When some leakage or deterioration in performance does occur after a *very* big mileage it is time to fit replacement rear-suspension units or get the manufacturers to service the internal mechanism of the faulty units. Should the springs become weak after a big mileage you can renew these yourself. You can also renew the rubber bushes fitted to the top and bottom eyes of the units, if renewal is called for. It is simple to push the old bushes out and press in new ones.

To obtain access to the springs of both rear-suspension units, the units should be removed from the frame after first removing the rear mudguard unit (*see* page 108). To remove the spring from each unit, push down the top cover so as to release the split collar above it. After removing the split collar lift off the top cover and withdraw the spring. Before fitting a new spring, grease it to prevent rust and also squeaking in the event of it contacting either of the covers.

INDEX

ACCESSORY firms, 59
Alignment, wheel, 105
Alternator, Lucas, 39

BATTERY charging, 38, 41
Battery maintenance, 40–4
Brake—
  adjustment, 103, 105
  shoes, 105
Bulbs, 45–7

CAM gear, dismantling, 89
Carburettor—
  assembling, 23
  dismantling, inspecting, 21
  settings, 25
Chain tension, secondary, 96
Chains, timing and primary, 64–7
Cleaning—
  chromium, 61
  contacts, 54
  enamelled parts, 61
  engine-gearbox unit, 61
  oil filters, 32
  silencer, 74
  sparking plugs, 50, 53
  suspension units, 37
Climbing hills, 10
Clutch—
  control, adjusting, 92
  plates, removing, 92
  slip, 92
Coil, ignition, 50
Colloidal graphite, 13
Connecting-rod bearings, 80
Connexions, battery terminal, 44
Contact breaker, 34, 53
Control layout, 4
Crankcase breather, 69
Cush-drive, 98–100
Cylinder—
  barrel, 74, 84
  head, 71, 84

DECARBONIZING, valve grinding, 69–87
Detergent oils, 31
Dipstick, 30
Draining—
  engine sump, 32
  oil tank, 32
Driving licence, 3
Dry-sump lubrication, 26

ENGINE—
  lubrication, 26–34
  oils, suitable, 30
  unit, removing, 91

FAIRING, 3
Filter—
  air, 25
  oil, 32
  petrol, 24

GAP—
  contact-breaker, 53
  piston ring, 78
  sparking plug, 50
Gear changing, 8–10
Gearbox maintenance, 34, 91
Greases, suitable, 36
Grinding-in valves, 82
Gudgeon-pin removal, 76

HILL climbing, 10
Horn trouble, 47

IGNITION—
  switch, 4
  timing, 55–8, 87–8
Inner tube, removing, 102
Internal oil pipes, 69

JET-NEEDLE, 16, 23

LAMPS, 44–7
Legal preliminaries, 1
Light unit, Lucas, 44

Lighting switch, 5, 38
Linings, brake, 103–5
Lubrication—
　brake, 37
　centre stand pivot, 37
　contact-breaker, 34
　dipper switch, 36
　engine, 26–34
　foot gear-change, 37
　front forks, 35
　gearbox, 34
　handlebar controls, 36
　primary chain, 34
　secondary chain, 35
　speedometer drive, 36
　steering-head bearings, 35
　wheel hubs, 36

MAIN jet, 15
Maintenance, items for, 60
Major engine overhaul, 89
"Monobloc" carburettor, 15–25
Multi-grade oils, 31

NEEDLE jet, 16, 23

OIL—
　circulation, 28, 29
　filters, cleaning, 32
　pressure relief valves, 34, 69
　pump, 26, 27, 68
　return, checking, 31
　return pump, 27
　tank, 30, 32
Overhead rockers, removing, 74

PARKING bulb, 46
Petrol—
　consumption, high, 20
　tank, removing, 70
Pilot—
　air-adjusting screw, 15
　jet obstructed, 20
Piston—
　removal, 75

Piston (*contd.*)—
　rings, 77, 79
　seizure, 13
"Pre-focus" main bulb, 45
Preliminaries, i
Pressure-control valve, 28

REAR suspension, 37, 117
Rectifier, Lucas, 39
Registration licence, 1
Riding position, 6
Rotor, 39
Running-in, 11

SAFETY, advice on, 13
Secondary chain, 35, 97
Slow-running, 19, 20
Spares and repairs, 59
Sparking plug—
　gap, 50
　replacing, 53
Sparking plugs, suitable, 49
Speedometer light, 47
Starting up, 7, 38
Stator, 39
Steering head, 35, 112
Stop-tail lamp, 46
Stopping, 10, 11

TELESCOPIC front forks, 35, 113–16
Testing plug and H.T. leads, 53
Throttle—
　stop, 15
　valve, 23
Tools, special, 60
Tyre pressures, 101

VALVE—
　and ignition timings, 87–8
　clearances, 62–3
　removal, 80
　springs, 82

WARMING-UP engine, 19, 31
Wheels, 105–11
Wiring diagrams, 57

ARE YOU:
INTERESTED IN EUROPEAN, IMPORT & EXOTIC AUTOMOBILES?

DO YOU:
DO YOUR OWN MAINTENANCE?

If you answered yes to either of these questions, then you should check out our automobile books and manuals. We have included a sample listing of some of our featured marques. However, for complete details and the most up-to-date information, please visit our website.

—— www.VelocePress.com ——

The fastest growing specialist USA publisher of niche market automotive books and manuals.

All VelocePress titles are available through your local independent bookseller, Amazon.com or direct from VelocePress. Wholesale customers may also purchase direct or from the Ingram Book Group.

AUTOBOOKS WORKSHOP MANUALS

ALFA ROMEO GIULIA 1300, 1600, 1750, 2000 1962-1978 WSM
AUSTIN HEALEY SPRITE, MG MIDGET 1958-1980 WSM
BMW 1600 1966-1973 WSM
BMW 2000 & 2002 1966-1976 WSM
BMW 2500, 2800, 3.0 & 3.3 1968-1977 WSM
BMW 316, 320, 320i 1975-1977 WSM
BMW 518, 520, 520i 1973-1981 WSM
FIAT 1100, 1100D, 1100R & 1200 1957-1969 WSM
FIAT 124 1966-1974 WSM
FIAT 124 SPORT 1966-1975 WSM
FIAT 125 & 125 SPECIAL 1967-1973 WSM
FIAT 126, 126L, 126 DV, 126/650 & 126/650 DV 1972-1982 WSM
FIAT 127 SALOON, SPECIAL & SPORT, 900, 1050 1971-1981 WSM
FIAT 128 1969-1982 WSM
FIAT 1300, 1500 1961-1967 WSM
FIAT 131 MIRAFIORI 1975-1982 WSM
FIAT 132 1972-1982 WSM
FIAT 500 1957-1973 WSM
FIAT 600, 600D & MULTIPLA 1955-1969 WSM
FIAT 850 1964-1972 WSM
JAGUAR E-TYPE 1961-1972 WSM
JAGUAR MK 1, 2 1955-1969 WSM
JAGUAR S TYPE, 420 1963-1968 WSM
JAGUAR XK 120, 140, 150 MK 7, 8, 9 1948-1961 WSM
LAND ROVER 1, 2 1948-1961 WSM
MERCEDES-BENZ 190 1959-1968 WSM
MERCEDES-BENZ 220/8 WSM
MERCEDES-BENZ 220B 1959-1965 WSM
MERCEDES-BENZ 230 1963-1968 WSM
MERCEDES-BENZ 250 1968-1972 WSM
MERCEDES-BENZ 280 1968-1972 WSM
MG MIDGET TA-TF 1936-1955 WSM
MINI 1959-1980 WSM
MORRIS MINOR 1952-1971 WSM
PEUGEOT 404 1960-1975 WSM
PORSCHE 911 1964-1973 WSM
PORSCHE 911 1970-1977 WSM
RENAULT 16 1965-1979 WSM
RENAULT 8, 10, 1100 1962-1971 WSM
ROVER 3500, 3500S 1968-1976 WSM
SUNBEAM RAPIER, ALPINE 1955-1965 WSM
TRIUMPH SPITFIRE, GT6, VITESSE 1962-1968 WSM
TRIUMPH TR2, TR3, TR3A 1952-1962 WSM
TRIUMPH TR4, TR4A 1961-1967 WSM
VOLKSWAGEN BEETLE 1968-1977 WSM

BROOKLANDS BOOKS & ROAD TEST PORTFOLIOS (RTP)

AC CARS 1904-2009
ALFA ROMEO 1920-1933 ROAD TEST PORTFOLIO
ALFA ROMEO 1934-1940 ROAD TEST PORTFOLIO
BRABHAM RALT HONDA THE RON TAURANAC STORY
BUGATTI TYPE 10 TO TYPE 40 ROAD TEST PORTFOLIO
BUGATTI TYPE 10 TO TYPE 251 ROAD TEST PORTFOLIO
BUGATTI TYPE 41 TO TYPE 55 ROAD TEST PORTFOLIO
BUGATTI TYPE 57 TO TYPE 251 ROAD TEST PORTFOLIO
DELAHAYE ROAD TEST PORTFOLIO
FERRARI ROAD CARS 1946-1956 ROAD TEST PORTFOLIO
FIAT 500 1936-1972 ROAD TEST PORTFOLIO
FIAT DINO ROAD TEST PORTFOLIO
HISPANO SUIZA ROAD TEST PORTFOLIO
HONDA ST1100/ST1300 PAN EUROPEAN 1990-2002 RTP
JAGUAR MK1 & MK2 ROAD TEST PORTFOLIO
LOTUS CORTINA ROAD TEST PORTFOLIO
MV AGUSTA F4 750 & 1000 1997-2007 ROAD TEST PORTFOLIO
TATRA CARS ROAD TEST PORTFOLIO

VELOCEPRESS AUTOMOBILE BOOKS & MANUALS

ABARTH BUYERS GUIDE
AUSTIN-HEALEY 6-CYLINDER WSM
BMW 600 LIMOUSINE FACTORY WSM
BMW 600 LIMOUSINE OWNERS HAND BOOK & SERVICE MANUAL
BMW ISETTA FACTORY WSM
BOOK OF THE CARRERA PANAMERICANA - MEXICAN ROAD RACE
DIALED IN - THE JAN OPPERMAN STORY
FERRARI 250/GT SERVICE AND MAINTENANCE
FERRARI 308 SERIES BUYER'S AND OWNER'S GUIDE
FERRARI BERLINETTA LUSSO
FERRARI BROCHURES AND SALES LITERATURE 1946-1967
FERRARI BROCHURES AND SALES LITERATURE 1968-1989
FERRARI GUIDE TO PERFORMANCE
FERRARI OPP, MAINTENANCE & SERVICE H/BOOKS 1948-1963
FERRARI OWNER'S HANDBOOK
FERRARI SERIAL NUMBERS PART I - ODD NUMBERS TO 21399
FERRARI SERIAL NUMBERS PART II - EVEN NUMBERS TO 1050
FERRARI SPYDER CALIFORNIA
FERRARI TUNING TIPS & MAINTENANCE TECHNIQUES
HOW TO BUILD A FIBERGLASS CAR
HOW TO BUILD A RACING CAR
IF HEMINGWAY HAD WRITTEN A RACING NOVEL
JAGUAR E-TYPE 3.8 & 4.2 WSM
LE MANS 24 (THE BOOK THAT THE FILM WAS BASED ON)
MASERATI BROCHURES AND SALES LITERATURE
MASERATI OWNER'S HANDBOOK
METROPOLITAN FACTORY WSM
MGA & MGB OWNERS HANDBOOK & WSM
OBERT'S FIAT GUIDE
PERFORMANCE TUNING THE SUNBEAM TIGER
PORSCHE 356 1948-1965 WSM
PORSCHE 912 WSM
SOUPING THE VOLKSWAGEN
TRIUMPH TR2, TR3, TR4 1953-1965 WSM
VEDA ORR'S NEW REVISED HOT ROD PICTORIAL
VOLKSWAGEN TRANSPORTER, TRUCKS, STATION WAGONS WSM
VOLVO 1944-1968 ALL MODELS WSM

VELOCEPRESS MOTORCYCLE BOOKS & MANUALS

AJS SINGLES 1955-65 350cc & 500cc (BOOK OF)
ARIEL 1939-1960 4 STROKE SINGLES (BOOK OF)
ARIEL MOTORCYCLES 1933-1951 WSM
ARIEL PREWAR MODELS 1932-1939 (BOOK OF)
BMW M/CYCLES R26 R27 (1956-1967) FACTORY WSM
BMW M/CYCLES R50 R50S R60 R69S (1955-1969) FACTORY WSM
BSA BANTAM (BOOK OF)
BSA OHV & SV SINGLES - 250cc 1954-1970 (BOOK OF)
BSA OHV & SV SINGLES 1945-54 250-600cc (BOOK OF)
BSA OHV SINGLES 350 & 500cc 1955-1967 (BOOK OF)
BSA PREWAR MODELS TO 1939 (BOOK OF)
BSA TWINS 1948-1962 (BOOK OF)
BSA TWINS 1962-1969 (SECOND BOOK OF)
DUCATI 160cc, 250cc & 350cc OHC MODELS FACTORY WSM
HONDA 50 ALL MODELS UP TO 1970 (BOOK OF)
HONDA 90 ALL MODELS UP TO 1966 (BOOK OF)
HONDA MOTORCYCLES 125-150 TWINS C/CS/CB/CA WSM
HONDA MOTORCYCLES 250-305 TWINS C/CS/CB WSM
HONDA MOTORCYCLES C100 SUPER CUB WSM
HONDA MOTORCYCLES C110 SPORT CUB 1962-1969 WSM
HONDA TWINS & SINGLES 50cc TO 305cc 1960-1966 (BOOK OF)
LAMBRETTA ALL 125 & 150cc MODELS 1947-1957 (BOOK OF)
LAMBRETTA LI & TV MODELS 1957-1970 (SECOND BOOK OF)
MATCHLESS 350 & 500cc SINGLES 1945-1956 (BOOK OF)
MATCHLESS 350 & 500cc SINGLES 1955-1966 (BOOK OF)
NORTON 1938-1956 (BOOK OF)
NORTON DOMINATOR TWINS 1955-1965 (BOOK OF)
NORTON MOTORCYCLES 1957-1970 FACTORY WSM
NORTON PREWAR MODELS 1932-1939 (BOOK OF)
ROYAL ENFIELD 736cc INTERCEPTOR FACTORY WSM
ROYAL ENFIELD 250cc & 350cc SINGLES 1958-1966 (SECOND BOOK OF)
SUZUKI 50cc & 80cc UP TO 1966 (BOOK OF)
SUZUKI T10 1963-1967 FACTORY WSM
SUZUKI T20 & T200 1965-1969 FACTORY WSM
TRIUMPH MOTORCYCLE 1935-1939 (BOOK OF)
TRIUMPH MOTORCYCLES 1937-1951 WSM
TRIUMPH MOTORCYCLES 1945-1955 FACTORY WSM
TRIUMPH TWINS 1956-1969 (BOOK OF)
VELOCETTE ALL SINGLES & TWINS 1925-1970 (BOOK OF)
VESPA 1951-1961 (BOOK OF)
VINCENT MOTORCYCLES 1935-1955 WSM

www.VelocePress.com

www.ingramcontent.com/pod-product-compliance
Lightning Source LLC
Chambersburg PA
CBHW070556170426
43201CB00012B/1858